Stop Going Around In Circles-You'll Just Wear Yourself Out

by

William G. Seavey

Bloomington, IN   Milton Keynes, UK

authorHOUSE®

AuthorHouse™
1663 Liberty Drive, Suite 200
Bloomington, IN 47403
www.authorhouse.com
Phone: 1-800-839-8640

AuthorHouse™ UK Ltd.
500 Avebury Boulevard
Central Milton Keynes, MK9 2BE
www.authorhouse.co.uk
Phone: 08001974150

This book is a work of non-fiction. Unless otherwise noted, the author and the publisher make no explicit guarantees as to the accuracy of the information contained in this book and in some cases, names of people and places have been altered to protect their privacy.

First published by AuthorHouse   2/26/2007

ISBN: 978-1-4259-8341-3 (sc)

Printed in the United States of America
Bloomington, Indiana

This book is printed on acid-free paper.

Dedication

This book is dedicated to those very special people who give meaning to my life, The Koepps and The Capps families. First, to my daughters, Kelly and Karen; second, to my son-in-law, Warren and Kevin, and finally; probably these should be first, my grandchildren, Beth, Fred, Kody and Kory. I love you guys. Thanks for loving me back.

Table of Contents

Introduction

This is the second book that I have written. The first was, "Journey to the Top". Both books are about going to the top. "The top of what," you ask. The top of whatever it is you feel is worthy of going that second mile. It could be in your career, family life, education, finances, business or any other worthy endeavor.

During the writing of these two books, I asked many people if they had ever been on a merry-go-round. The type of merry-go-round that keeps you going around in circles and you seem to be accomplishing little in life. Almost one hundred percent of them answered in the affirmative.

The vast majority of people I met (including myself) either had been, were on one today, or were going to be on the proverbial "merry-go-round" in the very near future if things didn't change. Therefore, I decided to offer help in getting as many people off their merry-go-rounds as I could by writing these books.

Over the past 75 years I have learned many God-given principles that work, if you will apply them. If you do not apply them, then they are nothing more than just words on a page and you will never reach the top. Most people stay on the same page, never turning to the next pages of their lives. They're always using the same old methods that have kept them in the valley of failure. The mountaintops were in plain view but they never got off the merry-go-round long enough to go to the top.

The problem arises in getting the people off the merry-go-rounds long enough to apply the principles found in my books. Sadly, many people prefer the "ride going nowhere" over the hard work that it will take to ever get to the top but the harsh reality of it all is that they are going nowhere! Another problem arises; they don't know they're going nowhere.

This book is a series of mini-lessons for living. There are more lessons and they will come in the following books. Learn well from the lessons and you will leave the merry-go-rounds of failure and head for higher ground.

My sincere hope is that you will get off the merry-go-rounds of life for at least long enough to read this book two to three times; apply the principles, make a decision to get off the ride going nowhere, and discipline yourself for the long haul to the top. It will be well worth it!

Pass this book on to a friend. If they're not your friend, make them one by sharing with them your mountain-top experiences!

Dr. Wm. G. Seavey
Founder - The Winners Circles Ministries

Note to the reader – Books are tools; useless, unless used for their intended purpose, which is to learn from and grow up and go up the ladder of success. The view is much better at the top.

A SPECIAL NOTE

To Louetta Powell who edited the manuscript for this book and to her family which I am sure were a great help. A job well done! This book would not be the book it is without you.

Chapter One

Get off Your Merry-Go-Round and Head for the Top

There is only one thing you get when you have stayed on a merry-go-round too long – DIZZY! Dr. B

This book is primarily about two things; mountains and merry-go-rounds. No, not the ones you ride but about the merry-go-rounds in life. We're not only going to talk about how you got on the proverbial merry-go-round but also about how to get off. There is also another area we'll need to talk about, and that is what to do after you get off the merry-go-round. There are some mountains to climb and in this book, I'll teach you how.

Why climb a mountain? Because of the view! On a merry-go-round you get to see the same view every time you make a round. Isn't it about time to realize you've been on the merry-go-round to long? Get ready! Hang on! You are about to get a better view of what God wants for you in your life. If you're ready, let's go to the top. Now, I'm not talking about climbing a physical mountain but achieving to greater heights beginning today and for the rest of your life. Start reaching for God's best in your life. He has a great plan for you and it isn't to ride merry-go-rounds the rest of your life. God wants you to go higher than you have ever been. He wants you off the merry-go-rounds and reaching for the top. What top? The top of anything you have the faith to believe Him for. It doesn't take faith to ride a merry-go-round but it does to believe God for His best in your life.

This book is also about stretching yourself beyond your comfort zone and going the second mile. Most people stay on the merry-go-round because it's easy and there is no challenge. It is a break for those who have gone through rough times. "I'll just get on this thing and ride until I am over the hurt from my past." You have no responsibilities while riding. All you have to do is get on and the merry-go-round does the rest. There is only one problem; it robs you of great potential.

Before we go any further, let's identify the tell-tale signs of a merry-go-round. If you are going nowhere fast, then you are on one. If there are no long term benefits, you are on one. If the ride is producing no fruit, you are on one. You have to know you are on a merry-go-round before you can get off.

What is the function of a merry-go-round? To go round in circles, offer a cheap ride, and a temporary thrill. If I get on, what will it do for me? It will do nothing of great importance. The ride has to end sometime. It may only cost a quarter to get on but it will cost you a fortune before you finally figure the ride was not worth it.

Ask yourself, "Should I get off this merry-go-round? If I should, how do I go about it?" If it's unproductive, yes, you should get off. The way you get off is to say, "STOP this thing and let me off. I'm tired of going around in circles." Have you ever noticed that the merry-go-round plays the same tune over and over? Here is a super success tip. If you do not like the music, CHANGE THE RECORD. (Record? Wow! That sure dates me!)

In my first book, "Journey to the Top", I talked about people who do nothing in life but go around in circles looking for an easy way to the top of the mountain. We called those mountains; achievements and successes. My goal for you in that book was to point you to the top and get you started on your success adventure.

My goal in this book is two-fold; to get you off the merry-go-round and point you toward the top. The rest is up to you. The top is a decision away.

I want to teach you how to have joy in the climb, not comfort on the merry-go-round. You will remain the same on the ride, but your journey to the top will change you. You cannot grow on a merry-go-round but you can while on your journey. Remember, it isn't so much about arriving as it is in the joy of the journey to the top. In your journey to the top, you will discover who you really are. You will discover hidden strengths, gifts, and talents. There is no telling who you will become once you start your success journey. People who are on merry-go-rounds are confused as to who they are. All you need to do is get off, and discover the real person on the inside.

Have you noticed that while on a merry-go-round you get to see the same view? Climbing to the top you get to see multiple views. You'll never weary on your journey to the top but you will if you continue to stay on your merry-go-round. A merry-go-round limits you to your God given potential. Climbing your specific mountain unleashes and unlocks your God-given potential and you can soar as high as you want. The key is "want to".

If there are principles for success then there are also principles for failure. Something must not be working for there to be so many people to be on the merry-go-rounds. We'll investigate those principles here in this book.

Have you noticed that the merry-go-rounds are quite crowded today? What with life's problems escalating, it's no wonder that they are crowded. But don't worry; there will be plenty of rides available. All you have to do is get on, but I am afraid the kind of merry-go-round I'm talking about will not be a joyful ride. There are thousands of people going around in circles not knowing how they got on the merry-go-round to begin with. Since they don't know how to get off the ride they settle for second best instead of God's best. The scary thing about this is that I've seen it in the Church where it should not be. I know because I have been in the Church for over 50 years and have that advantage.

What kind of merry-go-rounds are we talking about? How about these for starters: relational, financial, marital, sexual, addictions, religious, pornography, abuse, family values, and dieting. How about procrastination? Now that is a real merry-go-round. Those are the people who say, "Someday, someday I'll head for the top." Why not now? The answer most often is, "I'm just waiting on God to tell me when is the right time to go, then I'll move." God says, "Move, this is the right time!" But you say, "That must be the voice of the devil. Surely God doesn't want me to move now, does He? After all, I'm not really prepared to move just yet. I need to go round on the merry-go-round just one more time to be sure."

3

Most people who are on the merry-go-round have a dim view of
the top. The fogs of failure have rolled in and they have a dim view
of ever reaching the top. "Success couldn't possibly be mine. How
could it be? I'm not success material. I've failed too many times; I've
used up all my opportunities. Let someone else do it. God, don't
waste your time with me. I just don't have what it takes to get off
this merry-go-round." Well, you've got that part right. Most of us
don't, but God does. God is the answer to all our dilemmas. Yes,
even the merry-go-round has to give up its riders when God says
enough is enough.

When The World of Mirth Carnival would come to my home
town in Bath, Maine, I couldn't wait to go. One summer I actually
worked there doing odd jobs to earn my ticket and a few dollars for
the rides. The merry-go-round was the people's favorite ride. Well
actually, it was the favorite of the kids; the adults just rode along to
watch them. As a matter of fact, in those days (the 30's and 40's)
there were not many rides to choose from. The merry-go-round
always wound up on the list of favorites for most of those little
thrill seekers. The Ferris wheel would come in second place but the
same principle applies that I am laying ground for.

A Ferris wheel is much like the merry-go-round. It, too, has
its ups and downs. As the wheel turns there will be a time when
you are at the top and then at the bottom as it makes a full turn.
Life is like that for many people. One day you are on top and the
next you are on the bottom, but why not stay on top all the time?
You can, you know. You can stay on top of things even though the
world around you is going around in circles. How? Here is one way.
"*Casting all our care upon Him...*" First Peter 5:7 (NKJV) says this.
"*Casting all your care upon Him; for He cares for you.*" One translation
uses the word anxiety. If you cast it all on Him, then He has it and
you do not. See how easy that is?

Now you are free to get off the merry-go-round and head for
the top. The problem lies in the fact that we take back what we have
trusted Him for and try to solve it ourselves. We never really gave
it ALL to Him in the first place; we continue the ride going nowhere.
Isn't it amazing? One day we are on top and can see clearly. Our
footing is sure and we are headed for great things. The next day

our view is interrupted by unexpected circumstances and situations and we lose it. The fogs roll in and we lose sight of what we saw so clearly the day before. "I guess it wasn't meant to be", is our thought. The devil has won again. He stole our vision of the top. We need to realize who the real culprit is. He (the devil) has come to steal, kill and destroy (John 10:10). Once he has accomplished his goal(s), which is to get us off target, he moves on to other opportunities in which to kill steal and destroy. He wants to kill the spirit of winning which God has put inside of us. He wants to destroy our testimony of what God has done in our lives and he wants to steal the very joy that God has placed within us. Once he has accomplished those things (all three or any one of the three and in any order he chooses) we now head back for another merry-go-round ride. Once again, the fogs of failure roll in and surround us with doubt. Doubt is a killer. You cannot climb higher in life if you doubt you can. Look at James 1:6-8 (KJV). "*But let him ask in faith, nothing wavering: for he that wavereth is like a wave of the sea driven with the wind and tossed. For let not that man think that he shall receive any thing of the Lord. A double minded man is unstable in all his ways.*"

People who are on life's merry-go-rounds are unstable people. The Bible says if you doubt in one thing, then you are unstable in all things, especially if you have asked God for something and then doubt He can and will perform it in your life. When God shows you the next mountain to climb, go for it with everything you have. Don't stumble in unbelief. Don't procrastinate. Don't waiver; just go for it. When God reaches down to help you up, take His hand. You are not looking for a hand out. You are looking for a hand up; God's hand!

The truth of the matter is this; truth makes you free but only when you know it. John 8:32 (KJV) says, "*And ye shall know the truth, and the truth shall make you free.*" The truth is you can get off the merry-go-round. You do not have to endure this endless frustration any more. You can get off and you can do it NOW. It only takes one thing from you and it is this; you making the decision to get off.

One other favorite of mine as a youngster was to climb trees, rocks, hills, or anything else that would take me to the top where I could observe what I could not observe from ground level. "I wonder what's up there!" Away I would go, disregarding the caution of those just standing by. My mother would shout at me as I began the climb up my favorite tree in the back yard, "Better not go up there, William. You might fall and break something." "Yes, Mother dear," (I was such a polite kid in those days.) I would shout back, heeding not a word; just looking for a little adventure in a tree top. "I'm okay, I can climb this tree. I've done it before."

This book is not so much about the merry-go-rounds in life as it is about how to get off them and climb to a higher place, level, and dimension in life. God's purpose for your life and mine is not how long we can stay on the merry-go-round but to serve in the capacity for which we were created and destined. Riding life's merry-go-rounds requires little talent except to hang on and that is what most people are doing, barely. They are so out of control that hanging on to whatever is available seems like "Custer's Last Stand". But when we tire from hanging onto something we should never be hanging onto in the first place, we get flung into the abyss of calamity and chaos. After a time of healing from our fall, we get right back on the merry-go-round and go for another less than fruitful ride. The thrill for the moment is nothing compared to the bruises of the fall.

Marriage and divorce are like that and divorce is rampant in America. We get on the marriage band wagon with great gala and everything is great until something goes a direction we were not prepared for. A fight ensues and divorce follows. Not having learned from the first, we go into the second and the same thing happens, thus the proverbial merry-go-round.

What I want to teach you in this book is not only how to get off the merry-go-rounds, but how to climb to heights yet discovered. God has so much planned for you and me but we will not experience any of it until we get off the merry-go-round and head for the mountaintops. Why the mountaintops? Simply put, to find what is on the other side. What is on the other side of the mountaintop that I cannot see while standing at the base of the mountain looking up wondering? What adventure lies just over the top for me? What can I learn during my climb? What can I learn and become that I can share with others who are still on the merry-go-round? Who can I take with me and share great adventures while on the way? What will I become during the climb? How can I lead others to the top if I do not precede them and find out for myself? What testimony will I have if I do not climb to those heights God has ordained for me?

These and other questions are what you must ask of yourself to see the light at the end of the tunnel and get off your merry-go-round. Going around in circles serves no purpose. Climbing to the top of your every endeavor serves God's purpose for your life.

People who go round and round in circles are procrastinators. "Well, I've always wanted to write a book. Someday I will, I guess." "I've always wanted to write a song. Someday I will, I guess." "I've always wanted to be in business for myself. Someday I will, I guess." Someday never comes around and we continue the fruitless ride on the merry-go-round. What happens when the thrill is gone? "Well, I'll just ride it one more time." The problem is that eventually the thrill ceases to be. When the thrill is finally over, what then? For the most part, we are only looking for the next thrill. "Maybe this next marriage will be a better 'thrill' for me. The first did not thrill me too much. At first it was okay but then the thrill of it all was over. I'll just find another thrill." And we go for another ride on the ride without purpose. If your life's purpose is to thrill-seek only, you will lose in the end.

Then why go to the mountaintop? After all, it only has one top doesn't it? No, it doesn't. If you will look carefully at a mountain, you will see multiple tops. Go ahead and experience the thrill of climbing all of them because of what it will make of you and then go find some more mountains. You cannot run out of mountaintops but you can run out of merry-go-rounds. There are only just so many of them that you can ride. Merry-go-rounds are man's way of solving problems. God's way is to climb the next mountain. Mountaintops are God's opportunities for you to climb to higher places. When you looked at the mountain did you notice that the tops were at different heights? So it is with success and adventure. There are varying heights, plateaus, and dimensions to be reached and you will never experience the joy of reaching the top if you do not begin your climb upward today.

Have you noticed there are more people on merry-go-rounds than on mountaintops? Mountaintops can represent achievement.

To achieve something generally includes risk and that is where we lose most of the crowd. They will stand by and watch others climb, but not them. It is too risky. "Why would I want to climb that mountain? There is nothing up there for me anyway." Mountaintops are for those seeking higher grounds. Merry-go-rounds offer nothing but a ride going nowhere. It is a thrill for the moment. Climbing a mountain is an experience that will last for a life time.

There are no crowds on the mountaintops and there is no competition there either. It could get lonely for awhile until you bring others with you to the top. You've got to make up your mind to leave the crowds of naysayer at the bottom of the mountain. You may have to go it alone. Here is what God says about that in Joshua 1:9. (NASB) *"Have I not commanded you? Be strong and courageous! Do not tremble or be dismayed, for the Lord your God is with you wherever you go."* In other Scriptures it says, *"For where two or three are gathered together in My name, I am there in the midst of them."* (Matthew 18:20 NKJV) So you really don't have to go it alone. Take God with you.

People who are on merry-go-rounds seldom climb any mountains. They miss out on life's best. They've missed God's plan for their lives which is a better plan.

So many people are on the perpetual merry-go-round. They've been there for so long they hold title deed to it. It is their way of life. The problem is that they do not know how to get off. If you are going to climb higher in life, then you must be willing to get off your merry-go-round and it must be done today. You cannot afford another turn of the merry-go-round. Why? Because it goes nowhere, that's why. There is no end to it and if you do not take control, it (whatever that is to you) takes control.

Most of the people on their merry-go-round want to get off and go to the top or next level, (whatever that means to them) but they can't. They only get a glimpse of the top as the merry-go-round makes another round. Getting off is one thing. Going to the top is another. You know what happens when you get off a merry-go-round, especially if you have been on it for any length of time? You lose your sense of direction until you get your bearings as to your surroundings. You have to refocus and gain a sense of direction. Unfortunately, most people start off in the same direction they were headed before getting on the merry-go-round. If you are going to be successful in life you must get off your merry-go-round and head in another direction; that's called the top for those who have refocused. Otherwise, you will continue going around in circles. The old saying, "round and round she goes and where she stops nobody knows" is true today.

Most people stay on their merry-go-rounds waiting for their chance in life. No, life is not chance; it is choice. You can stay on or get off. It is your choice. Unfortunately, most people have been on a merry-go-round for so long they accept it as their way of life. When is the right time to get off? When you realize there are mountains to climb, places to go and things to do that are more important then just going around in circles all day long.

"How do I get off this merry-go-round," you ask. Wait until it STOPS. You cannot get off while it is still turning. Many try but it winds up being a disaster. Could it be that God has allowed some of the merry-go-round rides you've been on? Why would He do that? So you will learn something vital for your next climb to the top. You'd better hang on for the ride, but do wait until it stops. By then you should have learned your lesson (from God) well and you can begin your climb upward.

Only you can stop the ride you are on. All you have to do is say, "STOP! Enough is enough." Unfortunately, many return to their same dilemma as before. Proverbs 26:11 (NASB) tells us this. "*Like a dog that returns to its vomit, Is a fool who repeats his folly.*" God calls us fools when we return to that which caused failure to begin with. You need to find what caused the failure, solve that problem and never return to it again.

There are two kinds of people. Those who are on the merry-go-round and want to stay there and those who want to get off. Which are you? I can hear some of you saying, "But you have to get off at some point in time anyway, don't you?" Yes, you do, but will you? Take for instance, the battered wife who continues to go back for more beatings thinking that the husband will change. Think of the alcoholic who goes back for one more drink and continues to go round and round in his drunken stupor. Think of the drug addict who goes for another boost to make him or her feel better because life is such a merry-go-round. Think of the molestation that is rampant today. The merry-go-round continues because no one will say anything. The abuse continues because they would not get off the merry-go-round and climb to the next level.

> **SUCCESS KEY - If you will get off your merry-go-round and begin your climb to the next level as God directs your path; it will not be long until you will have made it to the top.**

You ask, "Then what?" Go find another mountain to climb and continue the process. Always be looking for another mountain to climb, not another merry-go-round to ride.

Chapter Two

Identifying the Top and Identifying with the Top

Now therefore give me this mountain, whereof the LORD spake in that day; for thou heardest in that day how the Anakims were there, and that the cities were great and fenced: if so be the LORD will be with me, then I shall be able to drive them out, as the LORD said.

(Joshua 14:12 KJV)

I applaud you for making the decision to get off the merry-go-round; now let's head for the top. Here is a key point. There is much to learn while on your journey to the top. The bigger your dreams, the more wisdom and knowledge you must learn. This is not a picnic you are on. This is about your life and reaching for the top. Learn well the first time. The second time gets a little rougher.

But first we must go through the identification process. If you can't identify the top, then how will know when you get there? Without proper identification, any place will do and that's why most people end up on merry-go-rounds. They don't properly identify with the top and success. Most identify with failure more than they do success.

> **SUCCESS KEY - It is not only about identifying the top, but how you and I identify *with* the top. Identity is very important but more especially, self identity.**

Give me that mountain (Joshua 14:12). You cannot have the mountain (success) until you have properly identified it and *with* it. I identify myself with The Enchanted Rock in Fredericksburg,

Texas, because I have climbed it so many times. It is part of me; it is part of my life's experiences. Identity opens the doors of access. It's much like a passport. It allows entrance (access) to places you could not go without it. If you do not identify with success, you cannot pass through the various stages of success. You will live a mediocre lifestyle and you will not attain to higher places. I must rightly identify myself at each level of the process; process equals progress. I must understand and identify the process in order to attain to the next levels. Ask yourself these questions as you climb higher. "Do I belong here? If so, why am I here? If not, why am I in a place I should not be? What is my purpose? What are my goals for my next level of achievement?"

You've heard people say, "Location, location, location." Here in this book, as we study climbing higher, it is identity, identity, identity. Know where you are at each step of the way. Know all there is about the next step, whatever that might be for you. Never be caught not knowing where you are going. You will only wind up in a place called, "any place will do". A road map is of no value if you do not know where you are going. You must first identify where it is you want to go and then the map tells you how to get there. The map is the process telling you how to get from point A to point B and so on. As you get to each point, you look back and see the progress you have made. "I've come this far. The rest of the trip will be much easier."

The identity I am talking about here is more about the identity of one's self. Who are you? For starters, you are not a failure. That in its self is worth its weight in gold. If you can get hold of that, it will make you free (John 8:32). Truth does that for a person. It liberates. When you know the truth about yourself (identifying with the top) success becomes easier; not easy, just easier. You will still have to fight for every inch of success. Knowing the truth means you no longer have a dimmed view of where you can go in life. You now have purpose and when there is purpose, there are no problems; just inconveniences and interruptions. Your approach to success is unhindered and you can go anywhere you want. You are not a failure because something did not turn out as expected. Failure is not a place or a person. It is simply an opportunity waiting to be turned around. You are not a failure because of where you came from or what you do not have (possessions). Your background (past failures) has nothing to do with your identity. Culture and race have nothing to do with it either. Your past should be the catalyst which propels you into your God-given destiny.

> **SUCCESS KEY -** **Identify your merry-go-round quickly but do not identify with your merry-go-round. You'll never get off if you do. People who identify with a poverty mind-set need never worry about wealth coming their way.**

I am not so much interested in the past of a person as I am about their future. I want to know where you are going, not about where you came from. "I came from the other side of the track." Ok, fine, but where are you going from there? When are you going to cross over?

The children of Israel had to "cross over" to get to their Promised Land. *"Moses my servant is dead; now therefore arise, go over this Jordan, thou, and all this people, unto the land which I do give to them, even to the children of Israel. Every place that the sole of your foot shall tread upon, that have I given unto you, as I said unto Moses."* (Joshua 1:2-3 KJV) Abraham was commanded to leave home in Genesis 12:4 (KJV)."*So Abram departed, as the LORD had spoken unto him; and Lot went with him: and Abram was seventy and five years old when he departed out of Haran.*" Both instances show a person leaving from where they were, to go to a place they had never been. If you have never been successful, you will have to cross over (from negative thinking) to the other side (positive thinking). Don't identify with the wrong mountains.

There are all kinds of mountains in a person's life; mountains of debt and mountains of defeat. At some point in time one has to leave those mountains behind them. It is obviously the wrong mountain. (See Deuteronomy 1:6)

If any one could have been a failure, I could. I was born out of wedlock with two other children. To this day I do not know who my biological father is. I was given away and became a ward of the state. I was taken in weeks later and at age three, adopted. I didn't find out about any of this until, by accident, at age sixteen. It was then that I found out that my Aunt Florence, who lived just a few miles from our house, was my biological mother. We never talked about it because I went into the military a few months later. I was married and divorced before I was twenty years old.

Failed relationships followed me every where I went. I drank for confidence. My biological mother and my adopted parents never told me that they loved me. There were never any father-son talks. There were no hugs from the mothers. For years I rode the proverbial merry-go-round searching for that ever elusive love I so desperately needed and could not find. I always saw myself at the foot of the mountains, never at the top.

Let's fast forward to the mid 80's. After another failed relationship, I moved into an apartment where I would spend the next twenty years shut up alone with God as had been prophesied by a man at a meeting in a local Houston church. After the move I "accidentally" (Yeah right - we call that a God thing) found a brochure listing motivational materials from several people. Zig Ziglar headed the list so I purchased a few audiotapes from him not knowing it was part of the plan God had for me as a speaker/teacher and writer. I received the tapes and listened to them while going through depression and migraine headaches that had baffled doctors for over two years. Even though I was suffering with depression, oppression (a bad mix) and severe migraines, I started writing. For the next twenty years I wrote and to this day have those manuscripts, most of which will be published in time. But it was not until I had identified with the top that I began to write with a desire to help others. My experiences would be the catalyst with which I would write personal development materials that would help others to the top. Notice, I did not say self-development. Self, void of God, is fruitless. Someone once said that experience is a great teacher if you can afford the tuition. It's been a tough uphill struggle but well worth the effort. Now I can look back at my experiences with a learning eye. They taught me what I can be, not what could have been. What I could have been, and should have been, (my past) are counterproductive thoughts. What I can be (future) is what I must focus on. You cannot climb a mountain backwards. Face the mountain (it holds your future) with your past behind you and go all the way. If you try to climb the mountain backward, facing your past, you will only relive the pain of the past, not the joy in your future.

In John Maxwell's book, Be All You Can Be, he pointed out that it is a challenge to stretch one's self beyond where you are right now. And stretch you must if you are ever going to achieve to greater heights. Ask yourself, "What do I want to be?" Here is one of my "want to be" goals; I want to be a person with enough resources to not only help myself but to help others. That is identification. Then ask yourself, "What do I not want to be?" For starters, I don't want to be broke. That, too, is identification. So many people identify with the wrong principles. If I do not want to be broke, what principles must I adopt as a lifestyle that will keep me from being broke?

When you get off the merry-go-round, you can get a much clearer view of the top. What is the top? It's your next achievement. Note: Don't forget to record your achievements in your daily journal and view them every day. Why? So you can track your progress. No matter how small they might be, achievements are important because they show progress and give direction. They are your road map to your destiny. The top is what you have accomplished with the opportunities presented. You invested your time, money, talents, and gifts and took it all the way to the top. The top is that place you have reached when you are through with your appointment here on earth. Look at it this way. Let the base or the foot of the mountain, represent your birth. Let the very top (achievements) represent your departure beyond this life. We call it the beginning and the end. What happened in between? There has to be a story about the in-between times. What did you do during that time? What's your story; your testimony as to what you have accomplished? Do you have a story about your successes or is it about your failures? How much time did you waste versus time used for God's purpose in your life?

On a tombstone you will find two dates separated by a dash. The dash represents the time spent between the two dates. Did you spend that time well? What will people say about you after you're gone? What legacy have you left for your family? What did you do during your life time that others will reap the benefits from?

DON'T LOSE YOUR IDENTITY – It can take you to places you would not, could not, ordinarily go.

We use name tags at various functions to tell others what our name is but it goes no farther. It only tells a person what my name is but nothing about who I really am. And unless I know who I really am, I will not identify with the top (achievements). I will be just another "name tag". I will live a mediocre life style, never reaching for anything above ground level. Remember, ground level is where the floods gather. It is where the problems are. You will find no floods or problems on the mountaintops.

I heard a person say this. "I don't want to become a millionaire. All I want is enough to pay my bills and have a little left over." She could not identify with more than enough. She only identified with barely enough because it was easy. She was unwilling to take a stand (make a stand) and say, "Enough is enough. I am going for more than enough." She identified with what was available to her at the foot of the mountain not knowing there was more at the top. She had not learned that there are more ditches at the foot of the mountain than at the top. In other words, she had a "ditch" mentality. She did not want to make the climb to millionaire status. Others could make the climb, but not her. It wasn't in the "cards" for her. If you are going to be successful and climb more mountains, you must have a "top" mentality versus a "dollar store" mentality. You must develop a wealth mentality and you cannot do that by visiting the dollar stores. Almost everyone can afford the dollar store. Stretch yourself and go to Neiman's every now and then. Why? Because it will stretch you. The "dollar store" mentality will rob you of the adventures of going to the top. This, of course, begins in the mind; see it in the mind first.

The Bible says in Deuteronomy 8:18 that it is the Lord who gives us the power to make wealth. You cannot make wealth nor have good success (Joshua 1:8) until you start climbing. It is life's assignment to climb. God never intended for us to hang around ditches or live under bridges. King's Kids don't do that; yet, in many cases we do. It is a lack of identification. Start working on the "wealth" mentality. It won't be too long until you'll leave the ditches and head for the mountaintops.

Have you noticed that when storms come, most of us will head for higher ground! Did you know that mentality was there all the time and that God created us with it in place? It came with the package. It is called survival. We can see ourselves above the floods if we head for higher grounds. Even a drowning animal will head for higher grounds. Where does the crook go that is running from the law? He heads for higher grounds. You've watched the movies where the perpetrator is running from the cops. He heads for the top. Why? That is where he sees safety.

Has anything significant ever happened on a mountain- top? Sure has!

Jesus was tempted on a mountain in Matthew 4:8.

The Sermon on the Mount was given in Matthew 5:1.

Prayer was offered in Matthew 14:23.

The transfiguration took place on a mountain in Matthew 17:1.

Prophecy was given in Matthew 24:3.

Agony prevailed in Matthew 26:30-31.

The ascension took place in Luke 24:50.

The law was given in Exodus 19:2-25.

Moses got a view of Canaan (The Promised Land) in Deuteronomy 34:1.

Abraham was tested in Genesis 22:1-12.

The Ark rested upon a mountain (Ararat) in Genesis 8:4. Figuratively, mountains are a place of God's protection in Isaiah 31:4.

A dwelling place in Isaiah 8:18.

A place of judgments in Jeremiah 13:16.

Great joy in Isaiah 44:23.

Great difficulties in Matthew 21:21.

Pride of man in Luke 3:5.

Supposed faith in 1 Corinthians 13:2.

Mountains were used as places of boundaries, hunting, warfare, protection, refuge, and assembly. Yes, great things do happen on mountaintops! Every one of these places represents at least one thing; the people had to climb to get there. To climb means you must leave where you are to get to a higher place.

START CLIMBING – Even if it is a little cloudy. The sun is shining somewhere. Go where THE LIGHT is. Stay away from darkness that your light might shine more brightly. *"Let your light so shine before men, that they may see your good works, and glorify your Father which is in heaven."* (Matthew 5:16 KJV)

Isn't it amazing the things we will and will not do because of a little bad weather? Rain, and not much of it, will keep most people from doing much of anything except stay in the house and watch another episode of how the world changes, or whatever the name of that show is. Of course, a good football game is an entirely different matter. Neither hell nor high water could keep us from missing a game, but watch the crowds dwindle at most churches when a little cloud appears. Okay, I've got your attention and stepped on a few toes, even my own. Ouch! That one hurt.

The top really looks good when it is a near perfect day. The sun is shining, the weather is beautiful, and the top (whatever that means to you) is in clear view and you want to go there. We are like curious little children who want to climb up on everything just to see what's up there. Curiosity makes us want to achieve to greater heights. There is no such thing as down to a small child whose curiosity says, "I'm climbing that thing no matter what my mother said." Risk, what's that to a small child whose curiosity has gotten the better of him or her? Just climb! Who knows what's up there?

As we get older our curiosity dwindles and dims and risk comes into the picture. Most of us would not dare make the climb in bad weather. If it were foggy we would wait until a more opportune time. If it were raining we would wait. If the top was not clear, we would wait for better visibility so we could see where we are going. There is nothing like being able to see where you are going. So why don't we go to the top of our mountain(s) more often? Why do we wait until everything is perfect? Why do we want to wait until the weather clears up? Why do we hesitate climbing to our destiny?

For most of us, it is because we want everything to be just right. We shouldn't take too many chances now, should we? Simply put, we don't want to take any chances or risks and we do not trust God enough for our sure footing.

So what do we do? We just make another circle around the foot of the mountain until everything is just right, that is, just right for us. And the ditch we have made from going around and around the mountain in search of the pathway that leads to the top only gets deeper. It doesn't take long until the ditch is so deep we lose sight of the mountain that God gave us to climb.

SUCCESS KEY: Don't major on bad weather for it will surely come. Major on the journey and what it will make of you.

If I think more about falling than I do climbing, I will fall more times than I get up. It won't take too many falls until I will stay down. Here is a key thought. When you do fall you only have to get up as far as your knees. That is a good opportunity to pray but few do that. Too many wait for 'good weather' before they will pray.

Sure, it would make sense to wait until a more favorable time to climb our mountain, but why not now? Sure, the weather has to be just right. After all, you can't climb to the top if you cannot see it, or can you? Maybe we can and don't realize it. Maybe it is a faith issue, not a "good weather" issue. Pilots don't wait for a perfect day. Many times it isn't perfect but they take-off anyway and you must do likewise. You cannot hang around the hangar all day. At some point in time you've got to take off for the mountaintops; or, you can stay in the hangar and just waste away.

The guy says, "Let's climb to the top of that hill over there." "What hill? I don't see any hill," you reply skeptically. "It's there, trust me. I've been there so just follow me," is the response. Just because you can't see the top doesn't mean that it doesn't exist.

The first time I climbed The Enchanted Rock in Fredericksburg, Texas; I stood at the foot of the mountain and said, "I am going to the top." What I meant was I was going to the top that I could see with my eyes. When I made it to the elevation that I had seen from the base of the mountain it wasn't the top at all. The highest elevation on the mountain was hidden from my view. It was behind what I had seen with my eyes. It wasn't visible from where I was standing so I had a little way to go to get to the actual top; the highest elevation. That is the way we are in real life. We will only go as far as we can see with our human eyes, not our faith eyes which will take us to heights unfathomable.

The ship must sail when given sailing orders but we want to stay anchored to our past which keeps us from sailing free on the seas of forgiveness and restoration. God wants to kick us out of our comfort zones, our nests, and learn to fly. For some it may mean learning to fly all over again after a less than favorable past.

"Well, what if I begin my climb and the fogs come and I cannot see where to put my foot for the next step up my ladder of success? What then, God? What are You going to do then? Will you leave me hanging, or will you come to my rescue and show me the next step(s) in life?"

God is not stupid. If He told you to go to the top, then you can for He has made a way where there is no way. So what if you can't see the top? God can! Our problem is that we cannot find the path leading to the top even though it is laid out for us by God Himself because we are looking for the path that does not exist. We call it the easy way up. We look at the top and say, "I sure wish I could get up there. Someday maybe I will but right now there's no way I can get up there. God, why don't you show me an easier way? If you will, then I'll go to the top. It will be much easier for me. After all, I've got this problem and it is keeping me from my destiny. I mean, just look at that pathway to the top you've chosen for me. It's too hard, it's too steep, and it's too rocky. There's no place to hang onto. What if I fail again? What if I fall? What if I stumble? What if I don't make it all the way to the top? Surely you don't think I can make it all the way up there, do you?"

> **SUCCESS KEY: If you are going to stumble, and you will, stumble forward, not backwards. Backwards is where you came from. Forward is where you are going; keep your momentum**

moving forward into your God-given destiny for which you were created. Anyone can go backwards. However, if you must go backwards, and some will, stay just long enough to pick up the pieces and move forward having learned from the your past. Get it together and move forward.

The what-ifs of life are what keep us from going all the way to the top. Get the what-ifs out of the way and you can go all the way to the top of anything your heart desires. There is no perfect time to go to the top of your mountain. If you're going to climb, then climb, baby, climb. The top is there waiting on you. Go for it and do it today. What if I do not know how to climb? God has not called you to something that you cannot do with His help. And that is the key; with His help!

The Israelites had a similar problem. In their exodus from Egypt to their Promised Land they went around and around in circles because they did not listen to God and follow His guidance and direction. He showed them the way but they decided to go their own way; another way. They chose their own path instead of the one that God had set before them. What should have taken less than two weeks turned out to be a journey of forty years. What a ridiculous waste of time when obedience was the key to the success of their journey.

Have you identified your Promised Land? Your promised land could be the next mountain to climb to get a better view of what God has planned for your life. It's no wonder the devil doesn't want you to climb out of your ditch or get off your merry-go-round.

Turn your ditches into trenches. A ditch is where the stench of failure lies. A trench is where you have "dug in" to make a stand to get out of your ditch. So, take a stand today. Make a trench out of your ditch and start your climb today.

Abraham was told by God to leave home and family in Genesis 12:1. Abraham said (paraphrased), "Where am I going?" God said, "Just leave the comfort of your home and family. I'll show you the way as you go." "Okay, God. I'll leave but You better stick close by because I don't know the way and I sure don't know where You want me to go. In other words, God, it isn't quite clear as to the where and the how of it all and I will need some help along the way." Abraham began his climb when, in fact, the way wasn't too clear.

The challenge that God has given us is the challenge to take a risk and climb the next mountain that He has assigned us. Why? Because of what it will make of us.

When the way isn't clear and we are stuck somewhere on our mountain, we must rely on God who laid out our life's pathway. When we do, we will be able to accomplish what God has called us to in a much shorter time. It will not take forty years. It might only take a couple of weeks. On the other hand, what God has called us to might just take forty years if we continue in our stubbornness to be disobedient to His instruction for our lives.

We go around and around the mountain looking for a way to the top; an easy way. When God points out a particular pathway to follow we pass it by saying, "Too hard, after all, I am only human. Who do you think I am? I can't do that. It will take too much out of me. I don't have that much time. I need to go to the top right now, today. I have no time to waste."

If we would follow God's pathway, we would get to the top much faster than if we had chosen our own way.

SUCCESS KEYS

- If we will get our minds off the pain of the climb, we will make it to the top every time.
- The top must be more important than what it took to get there.
- The focus must be on the top, one step at a time.
- Pain becomes manageable when we follow life's simple success keys.
- Focus on the pain and you lose your focus on the top.

There is a major problem that arises from going around in circles and it's called weariness. After all, how many times can you keep on going around in circles? We have not figured out yet that the results are always the same. We never find our way up out of the ditches of life. We never find the pathway to the top even though most of the time it is right there in front of us.

The Bible says we are to not grow weary in well doing for in due time we will get to the top of the mountain(s) that God has laid before us, (Author paraphrase) Gal. 6:9. The NASB Bible says we are to not lose heart in doing good.

When I climbed the Enchanted Rock in Fredericksburg, Texas, for the first time, I did not find the right pathway at first. And it is not always the pathway most traveled. Whatever pathway God has laid out for you and I is a very particular pathway. It is the only one that will lead you and me as individuals to the top of any mountain. It is God's prescription to the top for each individual. Remember, an aspirin is not a cure-all for everyone. It only works for some people.

By the time I had found the pathway to the top, I was already tired. I had spent over a half hour searching for the way up when all I had to do was follow the crowd. Most of them were not first timers like me. They knew the well traveled path to the top. CAUTION: There is a danger in following the crowd. Make sure you are following the right crowd of people. Make sure they are going the right direction. Make sure they are going to the top for the right reasons. Far too many people have followed the wrong crowd and wound up in a ditch instead of the top of the mountain. I know, I've been there and done that.

When following the crowd look ahead. Is Jesus leading? If so, that's a good crowd to follow.

People who go around in circles eventually grow weary and when God points out their pathway to them, they are too tired to begin the climb. They only make it up the mountain a few feet and cave in. A dog chases its tail for only so long. When it does not catch its own tail, it stops. The dog has grown weary of chasing something it cannot catch. So it is with people. We can go around in circles for only so long. The human spirit, mind, and body grow weary and we get tired of chasing the proverbial pot of gold at the end of the rainbow. When we lose sight of the goal, that is, God's goal for us, it is all over but the laying down. "I'm too tired. Let's rest for awhile. I cannot go any further." Be careful that you do not rest for too long. A little folding of the hands, a little rest, and the goal goes away. The view of the top of the mountain soon dims and you cease to see yourself at the top.

How many times can you spin in a circle? For most of us, not too many for we get dizzy and would topple over if we did not catch onto something to get some stability and stop the world from spinning around us. The same thing happens with people who go around in circles looking for the right pathway to the top. Eventually they get dizzy, that is, they lose focus and things grow dim.

Have you ever wanted to do the job all by yourself? I have. That way if anything goes wrong, you can only blame yourself. When my youngest grandson, Kory, was two years old he used to say, "Let me do it. I can do it. Let go so I can do it all by myself."
We won't accept any help until we get in a mess and even then we often times will not ask for help. Failure lurks just around the corner when we try to get out of our own messes. Some people won't ask for a helping hand. That's called pride. In climbing your mountain, whatever that means to you, you will need all the help you can get. You may make it part way up the mountain, but when the storms come, and they will, do not be afraid to just say, "Help! I need some help up in here!"

What is a mountain? It is that place in your life that is higher than where you are today. It is that seemingly insurmountable place that you want to go to but cannot for whatever reason. Your particular mountain could, in fact, be a ditch. Many people are in ditches. And those people who are going around in circles only dig the ditch deeper. It doesn't take long when going around in circles to dig yourself so deep in the ditch that you cannot see over the top. This is the insurmountable mountain of many today. There is only one way out of your ditch. Ask for God's help and you can overcome any ditch or mountain in life. What seems impossible to you is not with God.

A FROG STORY

A frog accidentally fell into an old abandoned well. He was knocked unconscious. When he came to, he looked up and said, "How am I going to get out of this mess?" While going around in circles trying to figure out how he was going to get out of his dilemma, the owners of the property happened by. Observing the deep well, they said, "We need to fill this well in. Kids could fall in and get hurt." So with shovels in hand they began to fill the well up with dirt. The first shovel full of dirt hit the frog. "Now wouldn't you know it? Here I am in this well and they are going to bury me in it." But as he continued going around in circles not knowing that as long as he stayed on top of the descending dirt being thrown in by the farmers, he was actually helping himself up out of his own dilemma. He quit going around in circles. As each shovel full of dirt came down the well, he simply stood on the top of the growing pile of dirt and eventually was free. He really didn't have to work on it. All he had to do was stay on top of things.

Here is another frog story. Two frogs fell into a huge bowl of cream. At first they panicked trying to get out of the bowl. Every time they would make some headway they would only slip back into the creamy goop made by their frantic attempts to get out of their predicament. Finally, one frog said to the other, "Man, I am too tired to try anymore. I can't make it. The harder I try, the more I fail. I am just going to give up." With that, he slipped into the depths of the cream never to be heard from again. The remaining frog tried all the harder. What he didn't realize was that in all his churning, the cream was fast becoming a bowl of butter. Seeing this the frog said, "I think I will just chill and churn around a bit. And with that he laid on his back and just swam around until the butter become a solid mass in the bowl and he was able to jump out of the bowl to freedom.

Now, why these frog stories? Here is what our first story tells us; you have to stay on top of things or you will get buried. If you stand still you will get buried but a moving target is very hard to hit. No matter what the world hands you, stay on top.

Our second story tells us that sometimes it just pays to lay back and get your "churn" on. Struggle often times digs the ditch deeper. Like a friend once said, "If you do not want to get deeper in your mess, stop digging."

How are you going to climb your mountain? How about this one? "I've got to see it, to believe it." Nope, as we say in Texas, that dog won't hunt. You've got to believe you have it BEFORE you see it; that is called faith. See yourself at the top before you ever begin your climb.

A friend from Panama City told me this story. Every day she would go to her favorite place on a secluded beach. Lying there all alone she would look upward scanning the blue skies for jets as they headed for America. She would say to herself, "Someday I am going to be on one of those jets. She finally made it after several years of dreaming her special dream. She would often fall asleep on that beach dreaming of the day she would be in America. Many had told her it was just wishful thinking but she knew better. She knew that if she could just see herself coming to America she would eventually have her dream. She has been in the States now for over ten years and enjoying every minute of it. She has even brought many of her family members here to her home. Those who said she couldn't have her dream are watching her do just that! What about you?

Chapter Three

Be Fully Alive

"I call heaven and earth to record this day against you, that I have set before you life and death, blessing and cursing: therefore choose life, that both thou and thy seed may live." (Deuteronomy 30:19 KJV)

What do you mean, be fully alive? Did you know that people who are alive to life climb higher than others? Those who do not climb or have no desire to climb higher, to achieve greater things for God, I call half-dead people. They are neither the fully alive nor the fully dead. They are the "Oh, woe is me" people. You will recognize them quickly because they are not climbers. They never seek anything above the mediocre. They live on barely get along street and refuse to move. They are dormant. Nothing is won but nothing is lost. They play it safe, fearful of taking responsibility. They never experience the miraculous.

Half dead people find life too easy to compromise and too difficult to confront. It means stagnation and living with mediocrity. It isn't death but it isn't life either.

Then there are others who have been beat up by life and have resolved to live in ditches the rest of their lives. They really don't care much about anything except that they have been "done wrong". There was a song out years ago that had that phrase in it, "someone done me wrong". They tell themselves they have no real reason to live so they'll just exist until something better comes along, whatever that is. For those people it probably will be just another ditch. They move from bad to worse by moving from one ditch to another.

SUCCESS KEY – What we really need is some people who will get down in the ditches with those who have deduced that life is unfair (to them) and get them out of those ditches

where they can see some sunshine (we should spell that Sonshine) and be useful people.

What exactly is half dead? Simply put, it is a person going nowhere fast.

To start with, let's look at a Bible story that references this phrase, half dead. In the KJV of the Bible you will find this phrase only once and it is in Luke 10:30. Here is the story in brief. A certain man was going down from Jerusalem to Jericho and he fell among robbers, and they stripped him and beat him and went off leaving him half dead.

Two people (at separate times) happened by the half dead man, looked at him, saw his condition, and went on their way. Compassion was not their cup of tea. Religion also played its part. Then a certain Samaritan passed by and stopped (compassion does this to a person). He rendered aid to the half dead man, bandaged up his wounds, put him on his beast and took him to a nearby Inn where he was cared for until he was fully recovered.

Now what has this got to do with getting out of life's ditches and climbing your mountain? The reason most people never climb their mountains is because they are half dead; halfway between death and life. You are neither fully dead nor fully alive. You are stuck. You are moving in neither direction. Ironically though, if you stay in one place long enough without moving, you will die. No, I am not talking about physical death. You will die without your dreams having been fulfilled. You will die without ever having achieved to any great dimension. You will die without anything, no achievements. You will not have been of service to man but at the expense of man, a person who was a taker but not a giver. Jesus said, "I have come that you might have life more abundantly." (See John 10:10) Deuteronomy 30:19 (KJV) says this, "*I call heaven and earth to record this day against you, that I have set before you life and death, blessing and cursing: therefore choose life, that both thou and thy seed may live.*"

Why would you choose a ditch (death) over life? The abundant life is available but so is death. Death is an end to things; life is the beginning of things. CHOOSE LIFE! You can't choose life in a ditch or on a merry-go-round.

On a scale of one to ten, where would you say you are? Are you more alive then dead or more dead than alive?

Our traveling man had been robbed, beaten and left for dead in a ditch (let's suppose it was a ditch for the time being) by those passing by. Though they saw his condition, they did not respond. In other words, they would not help him out of the ditch. If they did help it would mean they would have to get in the ditch with him. The man in the ditch had to climb up to get out and there was no one to help him. As he lay there I'm sure there was one thought that kept creeping through his mind. "How in the world do I get out of here and what did I do to get in here in the first place?" But this was his mountain, his calamity, trouble, misfortune, and his situation to extricate himself from but being half dead he could not do it alone. Those who passed him by obviously had other things to do rather than help this person who was down and out and desperately in need of help. They could have helped but chose not to because of circumstances that prevailed. We do not need to go into those here at this time for they will not serve the purpose intended.

Let's leave this story momentarily. We'll come back to it shortly. We've got to get the man out of the ditch.

A few years ago I was privileged to serve as a Police Chaplain for The Pasadena Police Department here in Texas. It was my custom to ride with an officer every weekend, sometimes doing a double shift.

One weekend we got a call to go to the scene of an accident about ten miles away. We learned via radio while speeding to the scene that a man had gotten drunk on a beach. While trying to drive off the beach and onto Nasa Road One in Clear Lake City, Texas, he drove into a deep ditch. The ditch was so deep that it practically hid the car from view, all except the rear bumper. The car was almost vertical in that ditch. By the time we had arrived, the drunk driver had extricated himself from his car and was trying to climb up the sides of the muddy and very slippery bank of the ditch. He was gaining no ground whatsoever. He would climb up a few feet then slide back down to the bottom. In his drunken condition, he was absolutely incapable of getting himself out of his situation, therefore, he needed help and no one was willing to get down in the ditch with him. Finally, the drunk resigned himself to just laying there and waiting his outcome, whatever that might be. I'm sure that by that time, he did not care. We finally got him out of the ditch, into the police cruiser and took him to jail. I saw him the next morning. He was covered with mud from head to toe and very hung over. To top it off, he had no idea where he was or how he got there.

The two stories are similar in many ways. Both men were in a ditch and could not get out on their own. Our traveler was in a ditch but not of his own choosing. Our drunk driver was in a ditch and it WAS of his own choosing. Both needed help, both were in need; both had resigned to whatever fate beheld them until someone might stop by and render aid. Our traveler was half dead and our drunken driver probably thought he was half dead, especially the next morning. They both probably felt that anything was better than being in a ditch, especially when you cannot get out on your own and no one will help you.

You've no doubt heard these phrases; "That poor man was barely alive," or, "she was nearly dead." When the two hurricanes, Katrina and Rita, hit Texas and Louisiana in 2005, there were people who were found barely alive. Some were more dead than alive. Some were barely hanging on to life.

To be between the two, life and death, is not a good place to be. You can't do much of anything; especially climb to higher heights.

You cannot do much of anything unless you are a fighter. The Apostle Paul was just such a fighter. In Acts 14:19-20 he was stoned (not with drugs but with rocks), drug out of the city and left for dead. However, in verse twenty, he arose and went right back into the fight. Here is the key; half dead people can come alive and be something if they do not zero in on their problems. Paul could have said, "Man, this stoning is for the birds. I'm outta here. I've had enough of this stuff. Life just isn't worth it. I'm quitting." But he did not do that. He got back into the fight. He dove head long into the battle and he did it with a winning attitude. "A few stones aren't keeping me out of this fight." The stones (problems) in one's life are generally what keep us from getting back into the fight. Even though the stones might hurt, it is only a temporary hurt. In 2 Corinthians 11:23-28 Paul talked about the problems he had been through. Notice the word, "through". He came through undaunted by problems. He simply saw something better than a ditch. He saw a prize before him. However, without the problems, he would never have seen the prize.

Here are just a few of the things that happened to him. He had been imprisoned, beaten times without number, often in danger of death, stoned, shipwrecked, dangers lurked everywhere, hardships, hungry, thirsty, and there were the daily pressures on him of concern for all the churches. Probably more than once, he hovered between life and death but he chose life and continued in his ministry. Though he may have been half-dead on many occasions he rose up even in the midst of some very serious problems and moved forward. He chose to forget what lay behind him, and moved forward to a higher place in Christ. *"Not as though I had already attained, either were already perfect: but I follow after, if that I may apprehend that for which also I am apprehended of Christ Jesus. Brethren, I count not myself to have apprehended: but this one thing I do, forgetting those things which are behind, and reaching forth unto those things which are before, I press toward the mark for the prize of the high calling of God in Christ Jesus.* (Philippians 3:12-14 KJV)

Being half dead is a place of no decision unless you see a much higher calling ahead of you. You must see the prize before you. Our man who had been left for dead in the ditch after being robbed and beaten was taken in by a stranger who saw more life in him than death. Our drunken driver saw nothing but bewilderment the next morning as he tried to sort out the problems before him. He saw no future; he saw no prize before him. There was no reason to leave his "half-dead" place in life. I would imagine that not having learned his lesson in life that he went right back doing the same thing he had done before that got him into the trouble. He went back to the ditches and the merry-go-round. He probably never went after the prize, a higher calling and a higher place than a ditch.

If you want to rise again to the challenges of life you must follow life's rules. You cannot turn to the right or the left and expect success to be handed you. (Joshua 1:6-9) Find the right pathway, climb to the top of your next mountain and with God's help you'll make it.

To surrender to the ditches in life avails nothing. With a winning attitude you can charge hell with a water pistol. David charged Goliath and took him down with a smooth stone even though others told him he was a fool to even try (1 Samuel 17:50). Caleb was 85 years old when he said, "*Give me that mountain*" in Joshua 14:12. Paul said, "*…but one thing I do: forgetting what lies behind and reaching forward to what lies ahead,*" (Philippians 3:13).

Half dead people don't attack their giants, they don't ask for mountains and they DO remember all that happened to them. They lack vision and see not the prize ahead.

Chapter Four

This One Thing I Do

"Brethren, I count not myself to have apprehended: but this one thing I do, forgetting those things which are behind, and reaching forth unto those things which are before," (Philippians 3:13 KJV)

Paul had the right idea. In Philippians 3:12-17, he lays out a plan that will carry him forward. As many times as I have read this and preached it, I don't believe I saw the word, "one", as I did the other day. It jumped out at me. This chapter is about that one thing Paul mentions in verse thirteen.

"*But one thing I do...*" This phrase takes us back to Luke 9:62 (NASB). But Jesus said to him, "*No one, after putting his hand to the plow and looking back, is fit for the kingdom of God.*"

One reason why people never make it to the top is that they keep looking back at their past. When you do that you turn your back to the future, which holds your prize. The failures of your past only produce more pain. Paul knew that. It is why he said, "I press forward for the prize." There are no prizes in the past but there are many in your future.

KEYS TO SUCCESS:

- You cannot go in two directions at the same time.
- You cannot think two thoughts at the same time.
- You cannot consistently act in a manner that is inconsistent with the way that you see yourself.
- You cannot see yourself as a failure while trying to climb your mountain.

Paul zeroed in on one thing, not two or three things, but one thing. It pays to have a single purpose. It pays to have a plan. (Proverbs 15:22, 16:3, 20:5, 20:18, 21:5)

There were three parts to Paul's plan. All plans have parts that make up the whole and lead to a destination. The parts are the process to progress.

> Part A: Forget the past
> Part B: Reach forward
> Part C: Obtain the prize

All three parts became the whole. It was the prize. Paul thought it to be the greatest of all things, to go forward and obtain the prize rather than bemoan his past.

The past hid the prize and Paul had to go through his past to obtain his prize which would be revealed in his future. By going through what he did, he was able to see clearly his future. I am sure that when he began his ministry he did not see the troubles he was to go through. He knew there would be problems but probably not to the extent that they had happened. It was only after he had gone through them that he was able to look back and see the fact that he had made it through; and therein lays the secret to making it to the top. You must GO THROUGH. Going through a thing is better than living in it or living with it.

You cannot move forward if you are constantly thinking about your past. Paul stood between two things, his past and his future. To do nothing would have produced nothing and he knew it. He had to make a choice. He could not serve God and his past at the same time. He knew he had to forget his past in order to press forward. The word "press" means to move forward regardless of the obstacles. I think he looked at it this way; if all life has to throw at me is imprisonment, a few beatings, danger of death, stoning, shipwrecks, dangers lurking everywhere, hardships, hunger, thirst and daily pressures, what else could possibly happen to me? You get toughened up to life when you have gone through the kinds of things Paul went through. Paul probably said, "Well, let's just see what the future holds for me. Let's get off the merry-go-round, get out of the ditch, and move forward. If I do nothing, God will get no glory from my life; so it's forward from this day on. What happened to me in the past is nothing compared to the prize waiting for me by moving forward."

Paul also knew it was impossible to forget his past. He simply made up his mind to not let it dominate his thinking. He wouldn't let it hamper his quest for the prize ahead. No one can totally forget their past. It is part of your life. But you can make the choice to not let it stop your progress in climbing your mountain, whatever that means to you.

Now about that past of yours, here is what I hear many of you saying, "I have no past because God has forgotten it." Now where did you get such an idea? Probably you are thinking of Isaiah chapter 43. If you think God cannot remember your past, read this chapter again. It has nothing to do with your past; it has everything to do with sin and transgression (Verse 25). Most people take this out of context making it a pretext. Timothy said we were to study, not read, as in a good storybook. Consider the following as you study the Word:

1. Who is doing the talking?
2. Who is he or she talking to?
3. What are they talking about?
4. Where are they (geographically)?
5. What time is it, before or after the Cross?
6. Are they Jew or Gentile, believer or non-believer?

Sort out Scripture this way and you stay in line with what it is saying and not saying.

You have a past. Deal with it!

Life is about learning. Paul said, *"Not that I speak in respect of want: for I have learned, in whatsoever state I am, therewith to be content."* (Philippians 4:11 KJV) What had he learned? That whatever state he was in at the time, the state of not enough or the state of more than enough, he found contentment to be the key. How long was he to be content? However long it took him to move into the next phase of his life. He learned that complaining was not a key to success.

Be content with where you are in life only long enough to learn from it and move up to the next level. The longer it takes you to learn a thing, the longer you will stay at the same level. Many people stay on the same level all their lives because they do not learn from their mistakes. Some people call there mistakes failures. I call them errors in judgment. There are many steps in life, all of which lead somewhere. If you do not move from one step up to the next, you will never find what those higher steps hold for you. Steps point upward but also downward. It all depends which direction you want to travel.

Paul decided to go upward for the prize. He knew the direction he was to travel for the prize. Do you?

Paul let the past lie where it should, in the past. He wasn't having a lapse of memory. He wasn't having a senior moment as I do sometimes. He knew his past still existed. But now having put his past behind him (out of sight, out of mind) he proceeded on to the next step of the plan which was to reach forward.

You cannot have anything in life unless you reach for it. Reaching denotes an action on your behalf. Little children who are too small to reach a thing will ask for someone else to get it, but we must grow up, we cannot remain as a child forever. If you have someone else reaching for your "stuff" all the time, you will gain nothing.

> **Success Key: Always reach for something that is a little out of your grasp. It will stretch you to your full potential. You will be able to reach only so far and then you must employ faith. Faith takes you to the places you cannot reach in the natural.**

Paul didn't have the prize yet but he kept on reaching. Forgetting his past enabled him to reach further than he could otherwise. His past would only serve as an unnecessary weight, a weight that would impede forward movement. Faith can't do its job when excess weight is holding you back. You must release that extra, unnecessary weight, and by doing so, it will catapult you into your future. (1st Peter 5:7)

Paul knew that what lay ahead was far better than what laid behind him. Paul did more than reach. In his reach he pressed. Pressing goes beyond the norm of things. That is why in getting off your merry-go-round, you must not only get off, but you must reach for higher grounds and beyond that, press forward. What does that mean? Most people give up when reaching because they do not succeed the first time in getting what they were reaching for. What they were reaching for and missed was not that important to go ahead and try again. It was not worth the press. What you are reaching for must be worth reaching for. It cannot be the mundane. It cannot be for one's self and gain. It must go beyond self. If I do not get what I was reaching for the first time, then I must press beyond my own capabilities. If it has worth, it will be well worth the press. With God's help I can press forward to that which I could not reach by myself. Now God gets into the picture. Now faith has come into play. Now I can do all things. (Philippians 4:13)

Paul was reaching for a prize. Prizes can come from having been in a race. Prizes come from having won a thing. Prizes come from having won in a contest or some sort of an event. Prizes come from the result of something. You open a box and there is a prize. Kids look for the prize in a box of cereal. So what are you after? What are you running for? Are you running from something or to something? What do you expect from life? Paul was reaching for the prize of his UPWARD call of God on his life. Paul had an attitude that said, "Let's move forward. I know what lies behind me. Why rehearse the same pain again? I've learned from it all, so forward is the only direction I take from now on." Here is a great question for you. What is your attitude? Are you reaching for the prize or are you still going around in circles still trying to figure out what life is all about?

People on merry-go-rounds are holding on as tightly as possible just trying to survive. They're hanging on for just one more turn of the wheel, but life is not about surviving. Life goes beyond surviving. Surviving is a natural thing. We are born with it. To get beyond surviving means taking a risk and stepping out into the unknown.

And to do that you must get off your merry-go-round. Now you are no longer in the survival mode. You are where you have never been before. You are in God's hands. He will show you the prize. He will help you on your way, the UPWARD way.

Chapter Five

Experience - A Great Teacher

*If you don't have a story to tell, how will others know how you got to
where you are?   Dr. B*

Someone said that experience is a great teacher if you can afford
the tuition. Life's experiences are your story as to how you arrived
to where you are today. No experience, no story. I've paid a very
high tuition over the years for my experiences, some of which were
unnecessary; or were they? Certainly every turn in the road, good
or bad, has brought us to today. Had we not made the turns we've
made, we probably would be somewhere else in life. Hopefully,
where you are right now is where you are supposed to be for God
to do in you all that needs to be done, to get you to where you
belong.

For those reading this book and thinking about wrong turns
made, know this; even wrong turns can be made right. God knows
every turn you've made and NO turn made by you or I took Him
by surprise. Here is a Scripture that will bring healing to those
wrong turns: *"And we know that God causes all things to work together
for good to those who love God, to those who are called according to His
purpose."* (Romans 8:28 NASB) The Amplified Bible says it this way:
*"We are assured and know that [God being a partner in their labor], all
things work together and are [fitting into a plan] for good to those who
love God and are called according to [His] design and purpose."*

Every turn, right or wrong, is a plan in the heart of God.
Sometimes we have to turn one way only to find there was a
better way. To correct a turn made wrong we just simply need to
retrace our steps and get back on the main road again. Remember
Philippians 3:13 which says in part, *"...forgetting what lies behind and
straining forward to what lies ahead..."* If it is lying behind us (failure)

then it is a dead thing. DO NOT mess with dead things else they contaminate what lies before us (our successes).

I normally do not write about myself but it is here in this chapter that I want to write about some of my experiences that have led me to writing and the publishing of many books. This particular book is the second of which I hope will be many, not because I want to write many books just for the sake of writing them, but because I have many experiences which I hope will help you up your particular mountain and on to higher grounds (Ecclesiastes 12:9-14).

It is amazing to me how the worst of experiences can ultimately lead one to where God really wants them. Sometimes the cost is tremendous.

When I began writing, I had just gone through another broken relationship. It was not the first, but one of many. My past was full of them. Twenty years later, I submitted my first book for publishing and now am writing the second book. There are dozens of manuscripts in my file cabinets; most of which will be published in the next years, should the Lord tarry.

The first manuscript that I wrote, "Adventures in Successful Living", was written during a time of tremendous depression and oppression. Sometimes we must go through those terrible times to find out what is on the other side. It all seemed to line up with God's purpose.

I had been in a particular church visiting many years ago in which a man gave me a rather long prophecy. It said, in part, that I was going to be shut up alone with God. Had I known it was going to be twenty years, I would have left church early, not staying for the good part of the prophecy. He said that God was going to take my ministry away from me, Discovery Ministry's, which He had already done, and grind me up until I was unrecognizable. He was going to grind up the wheat, the tares and the chaff until Bill Seavey no longer remained. There would be weeping and gnashing of teeth; there would be three terrible times. Hopefully, those have come and gone but the good part was this. He was going to hand my ministry back to me, The Winners Circle, and that I would be manna to the multitudes and certain signs and wonders, among other things, would follow my ministry. This is now happening as I write; the date is February 09, 2006.

There have been a multitude of merry-go-rounds during these twenty years. I'll write about a few of them here in this book. Hopefully, they will help you in reaching for your highest calling; God's calling.

This book is one of those merry-go-rounds. I had no written plan, only a title and a dream. Sometimes that might be all you need to get started. The first chapter was a nightmare. I rewrote it several times still going nowhere fast. Had I not put the brakes on and said, "Enough is enough," I would still be on the first chapter three months later. You've got to have a plan (Proverbs 15:22, 16:3, 20:5, 20:18, 21:5). Nothing was working until I formulated a plan. You must plan to get off the merry-go-rounds and climb to the next level. No plans and you stay where you are in life and you go nowhere fast. The trip that goes nowhere is very costly. You spin around in circles until one day you look up, and your life is over. All the merry-go-round rides were not worth it if you had gone nowhere. You paid to get on the ride and you will pay when you get off, if in fact, you ever do. But staying on the ride will also cost you if you have learned nothing. Nothing equals going nowhere.

Until just a few years ago, I had not dealt with the fact that I do not know my biological father's identity. It should have been dealt with many years ago but I chose to stay on the merry-go-round and not solve the problem. After 50 years of merry-go-rounds you would think it would be time to get off. One day I came to the realization that I had had nothing to do with the problem. I wasn't even around when two people, for whatever reason, got together and nine months later I popped into the world; and here I am 75 years later and still going strong. I might have been a product of rape, lust, love, or whatever; but it was not my fault. One day I just showed up, but rest assured of this; it was all in the plan of God. I might have been a "mistake" as the world would have seen it, an "Oh, Oh!", but in the eyes of God I was necessary to carry out the plan of God for my life and to be a help others. You, my friend, are necessary in the plan of God!

Many people are on merry-go-rounds and don't know it. And many more are on them and it isn't even their fault. Merry-go-rounds happen even to the best of people. How we respond is the key, not react, but respond. Reacting brings on more problems. Responding solves the problem. I know people who have beaten themselves up for most of their adult life and it was unnecessary. They thought the problem was their fault and it wasn't. It was their reaction to a problem, not their response to the problem.

Some people get on the relationship merry-go-round. They're looking for love but you can't find love on a merry-go-round. All it does is go around and around. And if you ride one of the horses on the merry-go-round, it goes up and down. That is the way many people do in their relationships, around and around, up and down. We get out of one sour relationship only to get in another. Our love life is just another roller coaster ride. We're up one day and down the next because we do not make sound decisions. After awhile, not knowing which way is up, we throw in the towel. Our fight for life has ended. Too many settle for anything and anyone to keep from facing real life issues. Real life can be found only in God, not a merry-go-round. Matthew 7:14 (KJV) reads, "*Because strait is the gate, and narrow is the way, which leadeth unto life, and few there be that find it.*" This is the reason most do not find life, real life. Are you looking for the straight and narrow path that leads to God or just another ride going nowhere? My mother used to tell me, "William, you better get on the straight and narrow." Little did I know then what she meant and so I went on many merry-go-round rides. The tuition was very high indeed. You cannot find THE WAY on a merry-go-round. You have to get off and focus on what is important. To most, the merry-go-round is just simply a way to run from life and this issue is in epidemic proportions. Those who are stressed often say, "If I can just get away from it all I can straighten this issue out. I can find the answers." So they go to a resort somewhere and hide their heads in the sand. They take the issue with them instead of giving it to God (1st Peter 5:7). It is just another merry-go-round. They come back to the same problems.

For years I rode this relationship merry-go-round. On my sixteenth birthday I found out I had been adopted but it was many years later before it really sunk in that I did not know my biological father's identity. If the story I heard from a family member only a few years ago was true, then I was adopted and raised by my uncle. He had two half brothers, one of which was reported to have been my biological father. I'll not attempt to go into detail here because it is very complicated. I've only sorted it out in the last ten years and even then, not completely.

The irony of it all is that there is a birth certificate laying in the vaults in Boston, Massachusetts, which has my father's name on it. Assuming, of course, that he chose to have it put on the certificate. It would take a court order to get that document and a lot of money. Maybe someday I'll pursue that issue. If he married, which I am sure he did, then I have brothers and sisters I'd like to meet. But for now at least, I am off the merry-go-round about that chapter in my life. I have faced it squarely and am working out the many details. This is the place where victory is won. There is a season in which God comes through for you. We'll talk about those seasons in another chapter.

Get in the race by getting off the ride that's going nowhere. Make a decision today that you are going to win in this race called life.

How about the religious merry-go-round? I've been in church for over 50 years beginning in 1931; not the same church, but all kinds of churches from the stricter denominational side to the much freer spirit filled churches and everything in between. There is nothing particularly wrong with that in that I had physically moved many times during those years. The amazing thing about this is that I saw the same faces in many of those same circles I had traveled. I'd go to 1st church and there would be Sam or Susie. I'd go to 2nd church in another part of town and there they would be, not together, but in the same circles. I'd go to another church and there one of them would be again. I left the denominational church and started going to a non-denominational church and they showed up again. They were doing what I was doing. The problem was that I did not know I was on a merry-go-round.

Scripture tells us to ask, seek, and knock, "*Ask, and it shall be given you; seek, and you will find; knock, and it shall be opened to you.*

For everyone who asks receives, and he who seeks finds, and to him that knocks it will be opened." (Matthew 7:7-8, NKJV) I find the word, "it" fascinating. It is the "it" we are looking for, whatever "it" is. Three times the word "it" appears in these two verses. Over the years I have heard this preached every way possible but no one told me what "it" was.

People who are on merry-go-rounds are looking for "it". Those people who were going around in circles (the Sam's and Susie's) including myself, were all looking for "it". I did what Scripture told me to do. I asked but no one had the answer. I was seeking but I did not know what I was seeking. I knocked until my knuckles were raw and bleeding, and still, no one told me what "it" was. Until we find out what our "it" is, we will continue our ride on the proverbial merry-go-round.

Unfortunately, many in leadership, including pastors in churches, are ill trained. They too, are looking for "it". Most of the pastors I have known over the years were looking for "it". Far too many never found "it" and quit. I know personally of five churches that closed their doors, still looking for "it".

Early on in my years as a believer (April 1976), and after a divorce, I asked my pastor what I was to do with my sex life. He said, "Give it to God." Not being totally satisfied with that answer, and certainly not understanding it, I went for a second opinion and asked another pastor a couple of years later the same question. He said, "Bill, you will have more problems with it because you have been married and are now single." My, my, my! What revelation! And I walked away from both of them not having found what "it" was and what havoc that played in my life as a believer.

"It" is an all-important word and you must find out what it means. To not do that, you will flop and flounder like a fish out of water.

What is "it"? It is that place in God where you find rest. *"Thou wilt keep him in perfect peace, whose mind is stayed on thee: because he trusteth in thee."* (Isaiah 26:3 KJV) The people on merry-go-rounds have not found peace. Peace is not the absence of struggle for struggle will always be around as long as there is life in you. It is what is found when you are at peace (in God) in spite of trouble knocking at your door. The answer to your troubles is, "Don't answer the door." If you do not want trouble, don't invite it. It comes without an invitation. How you handle it, is all-important.

Life is in front of you, not on a merry-go-round. Those things that so easily cause us to get off track are behind us. Those are the dead things yet we want to relive those dead things. We, who are not at peace, have a tendency to go back to the graves of our past and dig up the old to make it right, if in fact, we could. "I messed up way back there. I think I'll dig it up to see if I can redo it." No, you can't. Dead things are dead things and to toy with them is extremely dangerous. Put those old ghosts to rest once and for all. Be finished with where you were (past) and get ready for where you are to go. Bury it and do not exhume it again, for if you do, you will only unite with pain, not peace. Peace comes when dead things are put where dead things go - in the graves of our pasts. DIG A DEEP HOLE, BROTHER AND SISTER! DIG A DEEP HOLE! Their grasp is no more. You are free to embrace God and His peace. (Phil. 3:13, Is. 43:25-26) Struggle comes when you continually wrestle with dead things that cannot be revived or corrected. You can only learn from those experiences. Learn and put the thing in a deep hole and cover it up. Once the stench of the past (failure) is gone, you can recover from your merry-go-round rides and move forward in God. That is the place in which you can do all things (Philippians 4:13).

Chapter Six

Making Daily Course Corrections

"Only be thou strong and very courageous, that thou mayest observe to do according to all the law, which Moses my servant commanded thee: turn not from it to the right hand or to the left, that thou mayest prosper whithersoever thou goest." (Joshua 1:7 KJV)

Have you ever gotten off course? I have many times, especially as a student pilot. I started flying when I was about 14 years old and many are the times I got off course.

SUCCESS KEY: Know when you are off course and get back on it immediately.

Sounds simple enough, doesn't it? But it isn't when you have no guidance! Hopefully, in this book, I can help you get back on track.

How do you get off track? Let's examine a few simple things we do on almost a daily basis. You're on a diet and doing great. A friend drops buy with some homemade cookies. They just happen to be chocolate chip which is your very favorite. Now who can resist a warm chocolate chip cookie especially with an ice cold glass of milk (2% of course)? They're on your list of no-no's but an encouraging word from your friend pushes you over the edge. "Aw, go ahead and try just one. After all, one can't hurt you. I baked them especially for you." That does the trick. You eat just one. But they're so good you forget your diet and you have another. By the time your friend leaves, there are no more cookies left. The same things happen with smokers who want to quit. You forget the *promise you made to yourself* and in a weak moment light one up. Of course that leads to another "cancer stick" shortly after and you're hooked again. Alcohol is another area. You think, "Oh, what the heck, just one more for the road. What can it hurt?" Drugs are also on the list. We make promise after promise to ourselves only to break them time and time again. The list is endless of good intentions never to be fulfilled. It's a merry-go-round. Few ever get off long enough to examine the good things God has in store for them. It is so easy to get off your intended pathway, but good intentions never work. Disciplines and principles do.

You cannot get off course and treat it as a casual thing. The guy says, "I can get back on course any time I want." Sure you can, but it will cost you and the price you pay depends on how long you have been off course. I thought that way and wound up in no man's land. Getting back on course is not easy if you have been going the wrong way for very long. "Well, it's only a pound. I can take it off anytime I want to." Sure you can. The world is full of dreamers like you. If you do not think the first pound important enough to do something about it, the next few pounds won't matter either. "I can stop (you fill in the blank) anytime I want to." Sure, go ahead. Have another (you fill in the blank). Just be close enough to your grave so all they have to do is give you a little push and in you go. If you do not care that much about your life, then an early departure is eminent.

Now what has all that to do with making daily course corrections? If you leave this planet early because of habits not conducive to wise living, how will you know what was around the next bend in the road that you missed? How many lives (including your own) would have been changed?

Now I am not talking about you changing the lives of others. God hates it when you try to change His children to fit your own specific mold. I am talking about affecting change in your life that others will see as an example and change begins to take place in them. In other words, let God do His own thing. Keep your *hands off* God's part in the formula. Stick to what He instructs you to do. Too many fingers in the soup will spoil it.

In your pursuit of success, which according to Joshua 1:8, means to handle effectively the affairs of life or act wisely in the affairs of life, you must maintain course or failure will soon over take you and you will get lost. The intended course in your pursuit of success will soon diminish and it becomes another wrong turn in life. How many times have we all followed after the wrong course pointed out to us by friends, who themselves, are lost but don't know it?

Joshua 1:7 points out a principle, that when followed, means we reap the benefits of obedience. It says we are to NOT turn to the right or the left after we have been given certain directions. How else will you get to your destination if you do not follow directions? Directions are instructions as to how to get to a certain destination. To not follow those directions and instructions means we will not reap the benefits we would have reaped had we stayed on course. Failure is the result of disobedience of proven principles. Look at Joshua 1:2 with me. It says that Joshua and all the people were to arise and cross the Jordan. Verse three and four tell of the benefits. Verse seven tells us that in order to be successful we are to not turn to the right or the left. "The right and left of what?" you ask. It was the Book of the Law that had been given them. Verse eight says that they were to meditate on this Law day and night and that they should be careful to do all that was written in this Law and in doing so they would make their way prosperous and they would have success. The Amplified Bible says good success. There is success and there is good success. Which one do you want?

My mother would give me course directions. They were to the point and not to be disobeyed. "William, clean up your room." If I did as was instructed, the reward was generally movies Saturday afternoon, if not, no movies. It was as simple as that. Disobey course directions and you will lose every time.

You've got to learn how to read the roadmaps of life. I had just taken off from Hook's airport in my Cessna. It was a beautiful day for flying so I thought I would do a little instrument work to sharpen things up. To be able to fly an airplane had been a boyhood dream of mine and I actually started flying when I was fourteen years old. WWII came later and the introduction of those powerful, sleek, WWII fighters became my "special" love. Even today, I go to every air show I can find just to watch those old "war dogs" do their thing. The powerful engine of a Corsair at full throttle speeding down the runway is a thrill like no other.

Leaving the runway at Hooks, I turned west and climbed out to about 2500 feet. A few more zigzags and I was headed up north. I had a sectional map in my lap and was watching for familiar landmarks out of the left window that would tell me I was on course. Familiarity, that is, known landmarks, will always keep you on course. But what about traveling a course you've never been on before? I see several known landmarks. "Okay, there are the school buses and the school. Over there is that familiar church steeple. Aha, there is the old factory. It's still there after all those years. I've seen it dozens of times. Patting myself on the back, I announce to myself, "I'm still on course."

I'd been flying for perhaps an hour or so, a hundred miles give or take, and all of a sudden I saw something shimmering in the distance. Getting closer, I realized those shimmering objects at about two o'clock were lakes. Glancing at my sectional map, I didn't see any lakes, at least not on the course I thought I was flying, or had intended to fly. Whoa, back up Nellie! (Now how do you back up in an airplane in the air?) I was way off course! Now what? Fortunately, I wasn't that far off course and quickly made some corrections that got me back on course.

The point of it all is to never get off course in the first place. Life will hand you plenty of "bad course directions" so you must stay cognizant of where you are at all times. When you don't recognize the "landmarks", you might want to do a little investigating and see where you missed it. Let me explain what I mean by that.

What would happen if you asked for directions and you did not follow them, yet hoped you would arrive at your destination? Foolhardy, isn't it? "Aw, that guy doesn't know what he is talking about. You don't turn left where he said to turn, you turn right. I've never been this way before but any dummy knows you don't turn left there, you turn right. After all, I do have a very keen sense of direction." Now this is what a man would do. A woman would say, "We're lost. Let's ask for directions," and she would follow them to the letter arriving at her destination safely.

Many times I have asked for directions not hearing a word the person was saying to me. That's called not paying attention, but the person riding with me heard it all. I would ask her what he said and she would tell me word for word. "It sure doesn't sound right, but if you say so, let's give it a shot." And we would arrive at our destination.

If I had said course direction, we might not have a problem with that and go the new direction given. But for most, when we hear the word correction, it generally rubs us the wrong way, goes against the grain of things, and we buck and snort like an old mule that we are trying to make go in a direction it does not want to go. Like the words in an old song "Blue Eyes" (that's Frank Sinatra for those of you who are too young to know who Blue Eyes was) used to sing "I did it my way." We like to do things our way and when correction is given, we get our feathers ruffled, especially when the one doing the correcting is God. Course correction, however, is absolutely necessary if we are going to stay on track and reap the blessings already in store for us. It is amazing to me, how many times we will try to do it our way and then, when all else fails, we reluctantly do it God's way. It would have been so much easier to do it His way in the beginning. Think of all the pain you would have missed.

Course correction from God is not to prove how wrong we are, but how right He is. That is where we get our feathers ruffled. "Man, I messed up again. Wouldn't you know it? I should never have gotten out of bed this morning. Everything I've done so far has turned sour. Why can't I get it right just once? What's the use? I might as well quit trying." Know this; God is for us, not against us. Here is what He is against. He is against sin because He knows what it will do to us. So we need course correction. We just might get to our destinations if we follow right course corrections.

The Israelites wandered for forty years when it should have taken only a few days all because they did not follow course correction. They were told to not turn to the left or the right (course direction) but to go the way pointed out to them. They ignored the direction given and wasted valuable time. I wonder what their possibilities might have been if they had taken direction and correction to heart, knowing that God had their best interest at heart? You'll never know until you do it His way, and I don't mean ole Blue Eyes.

One of the things I was taught as a student pilot was to look for landmarks that would identify where I was and that I was on track. It sure made things easy. We were taught to constantly scan the horizon 180 degrees, scan instruments, and be constantly alert as to where we were in the air relative to the ground. Not doing so could get you in a heap of trouble. On one occasion, a helicopter seemingly came from nowhere on my left passing right in front of the nose of my aircraft. In fact, it came so close I could see the color of the pilot's eyes. That was too close. I've had other pilots flying multi-engine aircraft, fly under me and land while I was on final and set up to land. Sort of like the desperate tailgater that passes, cuts in front of you just so he (or she) can be in front. In another incident, a jet fighter came so close to my aircraft that his jet wash almost knocked me out of the sky. In all those cases, I never saw it coming.

SUCCESS KEY: You must know not only where you are, but where you are going.

The landmarks pointed out to me by my instructor were for my benefit. If I learned to recognize them as friendly, I stayed on track. But here is what happens to a lot of people. You're on the road headed for a much needed vacation. You've traveled this way before and know the route quite well. After a few hours of driving you start to get a little bored. A "Ho Hum" attitude begins to set in and you relax, sit back thinking things will work out okay. "After all, I've been this way so many times before, it's old hat to me. I never get lost. I see the school buses, the church, the sand pit, the courthouse and that red barn just off to my left. I've seen it a hundred times. Big deal!" You let your guard down for a while and all of a sudden you see an unfamiliar landmark. "Now how long has that been there? I've never seen it before. I guess I'd better check my map. I don't really need to though because I know where I am." "Now, let's see. That unfamiliar landmark I just saw is bound to be on this map somewhere." Of course, you don't have an up-to-date map and you can't find this "new" landmark. Actually, it is an old landmark, but being off course, you don't know that. You get frustrated. You check the fuel. "Umm..., not as much as I thought I had. Now, where am I?" Only when we realize that we are in danger of crashing are we willing to alter our courses.

Isn't that what most of us are asking? "Now where am I? I should be over there but I am here or maybe I'm here and I should be over there. I'm all mixed up as to where I am or should be."

SUCCESS KEY: Don't wait until the last minute to alter course directions; it could be too late. There might not be a way back.

The fiercest battles come from the mind. We wage war with self when we are being corrected, especially when we know beyond the shadow of doubt that we are right. "After all, I can't remember the last time I was wrong." Like a fellow once said. "I ain't always right but I ain't never wrong." What a mouth full that is! We have to have proof that we are wrong and even then, we will not surrender peaceably. "I'll fight until the bitter end", is the motto of many. Why then, the fight? Here's why. We do not want to admit there is that possibility we were wrong.

The real problem is that we fail to recognize we were off course. We thought the marriage would work but didn't bother to investigate those landmarks, alien to us. Had we looked into them early on, we would have been able to correct the course before it got us totally lost and unrecoverable. "I've been this way before. How could I be lost? How could I get this far off course?" And the farther we are off course, the harder it will be to get back on course. "I could have sworn this was the right way. Now it has all gone down the tubes. I just knew he was Mister Right. Now look what happened. Look where I am now; lost again." Here is a good word for you. You might be lost but God knows the way. All you have to do is ask. That's right; ask! Don't be ashamed or embarrassed because you got caught off course again. Repent, turn around, and get back on course. God is right where you left Him when you got off course. He isn't that hard to find. He is always available. You might say He is just a prayer away.

On a sectional aeronautical map, at least the old ones I have used, you will find certain corridors and elevations that you must fly in. FAA rules govern. You can't fly in just any old place. There are restrictions and limitations. Depending on what size your aircraft is and its speed, you are allowed in certain sky highways and no other. To get caught in a no-fly zone, is to have your ticket pulled.

Here is an example. You watch the news in the morning. Crime is rampant. But if you will notice, those crimes tend to happen in and around the same places, the "forbidden zones". If a person wanted to stay out of trouble, you would not want to go where trouble abounds.

A heinous crime was committed at a very popular club in a particular area of Houston, a nice area, not a dump. Did people stop going there because of the crime? No, even more showed up within two or three days after the crime. They had to be seen there. It would give them something to brag about. Trouble is nothing to brag about, especially when you might lose your life over it. Still, people run to those no-fly zones by the tens of thousands.

The problem with these no-fly zones is that we want to go there. Curiosity beckons us; calls us and away we go to those places we are not allowed. Who cares about the rules? It is the unfamiliar that challenges us. It is that forbidden place we must venture to find what lies beyond our restrictions. But when the rules tell us that we cannot go there, but yet we do, there are often severe consequences waiting us.

Here are some examples taken from Scripture of what it means to get off track.

Let's start with Psalm 1:1-6. It says that if we expect to be blessed, we must not walk in the counsel of the ungodly. And then it goes on to tell us more of what we must not do to reap the blessings of God. Verse three says if we do right things we will prosper in whatever we do. Blessings come as a result of doing what Scripture says. Consequences come as a result of not doing what God told us to do. This is how we get off track. So, we make daily course corrections according to the Word of God and we stay on track by doing so. We will receive more blessings than we could ever count. You remember the old hymn that goes something like, "Count your blessings name them one by one, count your blessings see what God has done..." You won't get to count very many blessings if you hang around the wrong people. That is what Psalm one is telling us.

The KJV of the Bible has the word "do" in it 1,368 times. It has the words "do not" only 90 times. Obviously we get to "DO" more of the things beneficial to us than those things not beneficial to us. God wants us to prosper.

Here is another example found in Joshua 1:7. The Israelites were told to not turn to the right or the left of the Law they had been given. The benefits included, among others, the Promised Land. The obvious is this; turn to the right or the left of what you know to be true and no Promised Land.

God gives benefits. Benefits are not earned; wages are. Benefits come along with the package God offers. He can take them away any time He chooses. It is according to the choices we make. Go in the no-fly zone and you lose your benefits.

Let's look at Deuteronomy 8:18-19. Read it for yourself. If you remember the Lord your God you will reap benefits. If you do not, you will perish.

Okay, you talked me into one or two more, read Deuteronomy chapter 28. It's about blessings and curses. Read Deuteronomy 30:15-20. It's about choosing life or death. Finally, let's read Deuteronomy chapter 6. All the above have the dos and do nots. If you make daily course corrections according to the Word of God, you will reap more than you could ever dream or imagine.

Now how do I recognize those landmarks? How do I stay on course? How do I recognize the "no-fly zones?" How do I get back on course? Here's how.

- Where there is no peace, you probably are in a no-fly zone.
- Where poverty (especially in the mind) abounds, you are off track.
- Where there is much confusion, you are in the wrong place.
- When the road you are on is leading nowhere, you are off track.

Off track means to be in an area not conducive to success; it is where the muck and mire are. It offers no "ease" of travel. It's like getting off a paved road onto an old dirt road. It just stirs up the dirt and dust. It's rugged and hard to travel. Get back on the "paved road", a level road, a road easily traveled when you follow the rules.

- You are off track when the majority is negative thinking.
- You are off track when you have no goals, ambitions, or want to do meaningful things.
- You are off track when you are going downhill and every one else is climbing to the top for a successful lifestyle.
- You are off track when opportunity eludes you all the time.

Read the Word of God daily to find out where you are missing it. It is your daily "directional guide" to quality living. There will be many corrections along the way, but those course corrections will be lifesavers to you. You will reap bountifully if you do not grow weary (Galatians 6:9). STAY ON TRACK! STAY OUT OF THE NO-FLY ZONES!

Chapter Seven

Watch Out! There's Alligators in the Jordan

As soon as all the people had finished crossing over, the ark of the LORD, and the priests, crossed over in front of the people. (Joshua 4:11)

If you and I are going to cross over from failure to success, we need to do it completely, leaving no stoned unturned. We cannot afford to stop midway. There are too many "gators" waiting for us.

Do you remember what the word success means in the Bible? That word only shows up once in the KJV of the Bible. It is found in Joshua 1:8. "*This book of the law shall not depart out of thy mouth; but thou shalt meditate therein day and night, that thou mayest observe to do according to all that is written therein: for then thou shalt make thy way prosperous, and then thou shalt have good success.*"

The word "success" means to act wisely in the affairs of life. Have you acted wisely in the affairs of your life? Hopefully, the answer is yes, but suffices it to say, I've missed a few along the way. I've been bitten by some of the "gators" who were just waiting for a good meal.

Too many people are trying to find an easy way to cross over the raging, torrential rivers of life. Many of those rivers, however, are just noisy, aggravating, and inconvenient little ditches filled with the stagnant waters of failure that we do not know how to "cross over". We're going around in circles trying to find Mr. Easy and he does not exist. We won't cross over because we are afraid of the "Alligators" in the river of opportunity.

The phrase, crossover, appears 26 times in the NIV Bible and 34 times in the NRSV of the Bible. Most of those verses are found in the Old Testament. Many of those verses are referring to the crossing over of the Jordan River. There is another phrase referring to crossing over and it is the phrase go-over. It appears 31 times in the KJV of the Bible and refers many times to the crossing over of the Jordan. To go-over means to leave where you are (failure) and go over to where opportunity awaits you. Opportunity does not move from one place to another, hoping you might catch up to it. No, you must go where it is. It will wait until you get there, wherever "there" is. It may be just across the river but watch out for the crocs and gators as you cross. All crossings are not easy. And not all crocs and gators are that ferocious either. When you cross over, use them to your advantage. Don't be afraid. Fear will cause you to stop halfway to examine the trip. That is when you are most vulnerable! Jump across the backs (failure) of those who have exposed themselves to hopefully scare you off. Or in other words, stay on top of it all. It would be like jumping from rock to rock to cross over. Don't let failure suck you under. Remember that all crocs and gators are not after you. There will be some, old and toothless, looking fierce, but are not. Use them for stepping-stones to make your way across. Advantage is wrapped up in failure and when unwrapped, it points you to your success pathway. Remember too, there are those reptiles that are inexperienced. Not all crocs and gators catch their prey. Just be careful that what they do catch is not you. Don't worry about the bluffers. They're all show! They growl a lot and bare their teeth but that is about as far as they will venture.

The Jordan River is about 200 miles long stretching from Mount Hermon to the Dead Sea. The Jordan starts in northern Israel at the foot of Mount Hermon more than 1,500 feet above sea level, and ends almost 1,400 feet below sea level at the Dead Sea. It flows from the Great Rift Valley, all the way to Lake Victoria in southern Africa. It is one of the fastest flowing rivers for its size in the world. The Jordan is only 50 to 75 feet across in most places. Today, it is dammed up where it runs out of the Sea of Galilee in order to meet the state of Israel's water needs.

Is there anything significant about the Jordan? Yes, there is. Here are a few of them.

- *The Jordan River was despised by foreigners in 2 Kings 5:10,12.*
- *Lot dwelt near the Jordan River in Genesis 13:8-13.*

- *Jacob crossed the river in Genesis 32:10.*
- *Moses was forbidden to cross the river in Deuteronomy 3:27.*
- *Israel crosses miraculously in Joshua, chapter 3.*
- *Stones commemorate the crossing in Joshua, chapter 4.*
- *David crosses in flight in 2 Samuel 17:22, 24.*
- *The river was divided by Elijah in 2 Kings 2:5-8.*
- *It was also divided by Elisha in 2 Kings 2:13-14.*
- *Naaman was healed in the river in 2 Kings 5:10, 14.*
- *John's baptism took place in Matthew 3:6.*
- *Jesus was baptized in the river according to Matthew 3:3-17.*

The Jordan River wasn't your everyday, ordinary river. Here are more facts about the River Jordan.

The Israelites saw it as a barrier that meant to them, it was something that had to be crossed. Before they could enter into the calling of God, they first had to cross over the barrier. You, too, must do likewise. Whatever barrier presents it's self, hindering your travel to what God has promised, must first be crossed. How else will you get to the other side?

The Jordan stood as an obstacle to their entry into the Promised Land. Obstacles in your life are God's assignment for you to conquer. If you do not conquer them, they will remain obstacles hindering you from everything God has planned for you.

They gained protection by crossing over the Jordan. It was an obstacle to overcome. They stepped out in faith despite the fear of the fast-flowing floodwaters. After their wanderings in the desert for forty years, they were ready to possess their Promised Land and they were anxious to get to the other side. But there was one last barrier and it was the raging Jordan, for it was at flood stage during this time (Joshua 3:15).

They had to cross over but to do so would mean having to step into the raging waters. They could no longer be spectators of the river. That meant faith had to be employed; great faith, for one missed step would plunge them into the floodwaters. They could either trust God's power or they could disobey God's direction for

58

their lives, which would mean failure. They were probably terrified but they took that initial step and when they did, God stopped the waters so that the Israelites could cross over (Joshua 3:16).

Rivers can be very treacherous, especially when they are full of alligators. What do I mean by that? Here are a few of those alligators. Fear, afraid of taking a risk, fear of failing, looking to our past, fear of what people might say, fear of rejection, fear of not "measuring up" generally to the standards of others, and the list is endless. Alligators get into your relationships and into your marriage. They get into the work place. They are even found in the Church. They'll show up any place where there is a potential meal. That meal, of course, is you and I.

Alligators are ruthless, especially when hungry, which seems to be all the time. When there is a migration of wild animals that have to cross crocodile or alligator infested rivers, there is little chance for those animals that are very young, that are sickly, or that tarry. If the alligator can get a good grip on you, it's over. Once they get a grip on you, they pull you under the waters to drown you while ripping you apart. It is not a pleasant way to die.

Alligators are cunning; they lie low waiting to pounce on you for their next meal. They lie in shallow waters undetected. When you are the least aware of them is when they attack. They can lie in the murky depths of the shallowest of waters, even in the mud, and if you pass by too close, your dinner.

SUCCESS KEY: Never get to close to a hungry alligator.

If fear can get a grip on you, it will pull you under its load and drown you into its sea of forgetfulness, and there goes your dream. Fear can keep you from crossing over to your Promised Land. You might only get to see it from a distance, if fear has its way.

I've seen just a trickle of water, called a stream, brook, or creek; swell into raging swollen waters from a storm, which has unleashed its fury. Fear is like that. What might seem to be just a passing fear, if left unattended, can get you into those swollen, raging waters called The River of Defeat and end it all. You and I do not stand a chance in those raging waters. When you find your way over, cross quickly else you will get pulled under by others whose only intentions with their negative opinions of your endeavors is to drown the very dream and vision out of your life. They stand safely on the banks of the swollen waters hurling insult after insult at you while you are gasping for air simply wanting to cross over to get your "stuff". It's tragic to see a person drowning, desperately clutching on to one last bit of hope, one last ray of sunshine while the "alligators" are having a field day. Find your place and cross over today, my friend. Cross while the alligators are asleep. Cross while they are off guard. Cross while they are having lunch (on somebody other than you). But whatever you do, cross over today! Don't let the "gators" get their eye on you for their next meal. Once they get a whiff of a meal, any meal, fresh or not, alive or dead, they are on it like a bass on a June bug. Who cares if its leftovers? Who cares if it is a day or two old or older? It all looks good when they are hungry.

Believe it or not, there are alligators (called antagonists) even on the highways. You'll notice them as they tailgate you on their way to work, nippin' at your rear bumper. I think some even follow us to the work place. One of your fellow workers rips into you for apparently no reason at all. You are his next meal! He has had no sleep for most of the night. The kids were sick, the wife wasn't feeling too hot either and things have not gone well with him. You are his next meal. He's got to take his frustration out on someone. It might as well be you.

Believe it or not, when I lived in Florida, I actually had to stop on several occasions to let a gator cross in front of me before I could continue my drive.

Your employer gets a piece of the action. You get home and the "little woman" gets the rest of you. Then there is the devil. I'm going to give him only minimal room here in this book. He is much like those alligators we spoke of in the river waiting for his next meal and it might as well be you. If you tarry in the rivers of defeat he will get you. But if you cross over quickly while he is thinking it over and getting ready to have dinner (you), you will have won.

Here is a real alligator problem. I have many of them in my past and so do you (if you are honest with yourself). One of the sad things we do is to cross back over the rivers we have just crossed and retreat into our past. But if you fought "gators" to cross over into your Promised Land, why would you cross back over to give them another chance at you? Yet, we do. We cross back over into the sea of defeat never to see our Promised Land. Believe me when I tell you that the alligators that were in your past are still there. That is why you were moving toward your Promised Land, to leave those guys behind. Who needs them? So why would you go back to be eaten alive? And believe me, again, when I tell you that those alligators in your past will be even hungrier when they see you returning. They will put on their bibs and gather up their utensils, sit down, and wait for their meal, YOU! Realize this. It is the same distance back to where you were (your past) as it is from where you were to where you are right now. It's a two-edge sword. It will get you in both directions if you are not careful. Why waste the time going forward in your life if all you are going to do is retreat to where you came from? It's called spinning your wheels. It is not only painful moving out of the ditches of life to your Promised Land, especially if you've been there a long time, but it's even more painful moving back to the ditches.

SUCCESS KEY: **If you move back into the infested swamps of your past, you will become infected and that will affect all forward movement into your Promised Land.**

There are only alligators on this side of the waters. There are none in your Promised Land. Here (past) is where the battle rages, there (future) is where the blessings are. Here you are faced with all your enemies. Over there, they are behind you. Put distance between you and your alligators. You know who they are. They are those who have been given special assignments to drown you; they've come to make you their meal. They've come to spy you out to see if you are ripe for the picking. Don't let them get a grip on you. Don't let them even get close to you. When it's their "snack time" don't join in their festivities.

I had one particular "gator" chasing me for a long time. He got a few "licks" in, but I eventually out ran him. As I told you earlier, I had been born out of wedlock with two other children and was given away at birth. I became a ward of the state until, at age three, I was adopted. Having learned at age sixteen that my Aunt Florence was actually my biological mother, I had many years ahead of wrestling with this newfound information (gator). Deep depression and oppression came. They knocked on the door of my frustration not knowing who my real dad was, and I let them in. The wrestling continued. It has only been within the last few years that I have come to the conclusion that it was not my fault.

Have you noticed that alligators are generally found in groups? When a meal comes by, they all join in for the best parts. If it were only one "gator" we might have a chance at winning, but when they attack you in groups and in force, as they so often do, it's a tough job fighting them off. You generally do not win.

Now, how do we recognize these alligators? What do they look like? Are they easily detected? If detected, can we escape them? How do we escape them? Will they come all at once, or, one at a time?

Anyone who causes you to divert from your God directed course is a "gator". What do they look like? They look like everyday people, just like you and me. You have to know them by the Spirit and by their fruit, or lack of fruit. Talk to God about them. He can reveal their true nature and intent. Listen to the voice of God for direction. There will always be the "gator" that gets a good "lick" in every now and then. Learn from those mistakes. When you get too close, you are his next meal. Stay away from those who mean you harm (Psalm 1:1). Fight those alligators off with the Word of God and prayer.

They might come one at a time or all at once. It depends how close you are to winning. The closer you get to your Promised Land, the more "gators" show up for their next meal. Point your finger at them and say, "Not today, sucker. Not today or any other day."

My major concern is that most people would not, could not, and do not, recognize the alligators in life until they have taken a bite out of them. Those bites hurt and can drive people to retreating from life. Of course you have figured out by now that I am not talking about those reptilian creatures found in the swamps of Louisiana. I am talking about people, situations and circumstances, all of which can take a major chunk out of you if you are not careful. This is all the more reason to cross over to your Promised Land.

Some people, especially those who have gone through relational turmoil, have huge gaping holes in their lives because of the gators. Huge chunks of their lives are missing.

Yes, it is time to cross over. You and I have been going around in circles long enough. It is time to stop evading the gators (past performance) and go over in spite of them. Distance dims failure. We've stayed long enough on the mountain of doubt wondering if we should go or postpone the trip. (See Deuteronomy 1:6; 2:3) It is time to arise and cross over. (Deuteronomy 2:13) What we may perceive to be a mighty raging river, many times, is only a small brook. It is time to possess, not be possessed with doubt and fear that we might not make it over to our Promised Land. The word possess is used 106 times in the KJV of the Bible, 103 times of which, are found in the Old Testament. Fifty eight times this word is found just in the two books of Deuteronomy and Joshua, both of which deal in part, with the crossing over of the Jordan River.

WISDOM KEY: You will never find your way to the Promised Land (success) if all you do is circle your mountain of defeat and failure, wondering if you will ever make it. Here is what the Bible says in Deuteronomy 2:3 (NASB). "You have circled this mountain long enough. Now turn..."

WISDOM KEY: Don't stay too long on your mountain of failure (past). You'll just wear yourself out. Here is what the Bible says about that in Deuteronomy 1:6-7 (NASB). "You

have stayed long enough at this mountain. Turn…"

Both verses of Scripture tell us not to tarry too long in our journey. There will come a time in which we must "turn", meaning turning from where we were (past) to where we want to go; where God wants us to go. Make up your mind to turn now. If the direction you have been traveling isn't working, then it must be time to turn. The Bible says we are to turn from our wicked ways. Turn away from defeat and discouragement, failure and disappointment, and head another direction. This time though, let the Lord lead you. Most of our problems come as a result of self-leadership, not the Lord's leadership.

Far too many Christians, however, cross over but think it wrong to possess anything since having taken a vow of poverty, if there were such a thing. Maybe in some religions there is, but I don't see it in my Bible or for me. I've made a vow to cross over and possess my "stuff" even if it hair-lips the entire world. Here is a bit of wisdom for you. I want to possess my possessions but I do not want my possessions to possess me. They're tools to be used to help others. As a result of that, I too, receive help. It is called the Law of Mutual Exchange.

There are two sides to every river. You cannot stand on both sides at the same time. There is the left bank and the right bank and there is mid-stream (indecision). Where you stand tells something about you. You can stand in the middle of your mess and go nowhere but that only makes things worse. Indecision never brings success; it only brings more indecision, and the alligators move in for the kill. Hesitation, many times, is the permission calamity and chaos needs to move in your direction. To hesitate as to which side I belong on is to invite the "gators" of life to a meal. If you are caught in mid-stream at least find a safe place to stand while searching for the answers. Don't let the tides of defeat rise, gathering momentum to sweep you into the rivers of despair. Plan on how you are going to get from one side to the other. Make sure there are no loopholes because that is where the devil lurks; in the loopholes. If you do make it only part way, make sure there is en escape clause allowing you to retreat to the banks you just left. This is the only time I recommend retreating, but be very careful, it could be used against you. It's not retreating as one who has failed, it is going back to make another leap at opportunity.

Remember, you cannot cross a chasm in two small leaps; you'll crash mid-way. Going back to your starting point, knowing full well you are going over, is to take another look at your plan; to gain advantage over the loopholes in the plan. Not all plans are perfect. Go back to the starting place and get another look to see if there is another way to cross over. You may have misunderstood the directions given. Maybe you heard incorrectly the first time. Maybe you heard "left" instead of "right". Retreating is not permission for failure. It is a "regrouping" to formulate that part of the plan you had left out. Maybe no one told you about the "gators". They said, "Hey, it's a snap. Just cross over right here and you will be okay." The trouble with that little bit of information is that they left one part out. They did not tell you about the "gators". They had never crossed this way before. They used you to test the waters for possible "gators".

Formulate a plan. Without a plan you will fail. Work the plan in your mind, "Let's see, if I cross over here I should be okay. Next, I'll go over to that spot and then to the next one right over there. So far, so good, but how do I get over there to that next spot? Whoops, that won't work! I've gotta retrace my steps. Where did I go wrong? Where should I have taken a right instead of a left? Oh, I see it. There is where I messed up." This is called course correction. Making the corrections before you cross over could save you a lot of headaches. That is why so many people fail in life. They had no plans; they just jumped in, and the gators had dinner.

If you and I stay on the wrong side of the Jordan, we will miss God's best for our lives. Everyone has a Jordan River to cross. When will you cross over? When will you get your feet wet? When will you step out in faith, knowing that God has your back?

The Israelites had to cross over where God told them to cross. Most of us want to find an easier way. "Let's go upstream or downstream. There has to be an easier way." Easy does not teach us. It spoils us because we are always looking for an easy way. There are no easy ways except to be an obedient servant of God. When you are obedient to God's way of doing things, easy doesn't come every day, but it sure is better than those old "gators" eyeballing you for their next meal. Do it God's way and stop feeding the alligators.

Chapter Eight

Give Me That Mountain

Now therefore give me this mountain, whereof the LORD spake in that day; for thou heardest in that day how the Anakims were there, and that the cities were great and fenced: if so be the LORD will be with me, then I shall be able to drive them out, as the LORD said. (Joshua 14:12 KJV)

Stop going around in circles and take your mountain. Take possession! Go get it! Make a decision today that you are going to stop procrastinating and take what's yours. If God said it's yours, then go get it. But for some people, if a million dollars lay on the ground in front of them, they would not bend over and pick it up. "Wow, man. That can't be mine. After all, who would give me a million dollars?" And we would continue to go around in circles wondering if we should, or should not, pick it up. Then, when it dawned on us that opportunity was right there in front of us, we would be too tired and weary from going around in circles to pick it up and another opportunity passes us by. Devil one, Christian zero! We've given another opportunity away to the devil.

Too many Christians are afraid of success and it is because that thought is based on religion (man's thoughts, not God's) taught over the years (Isaiah. 55:8-12). They do not know the truth. You can be told the truth, but until you know the truth it will do nothing (John 8:32). People are afraid to climb any mountains (God's assignments) because the Lord might "get on them" if they do. What a lie! So we continue to go around in circles hoping to find a way up our mountain and out of the ditches. Yet, religion keeps us in the ditch and the dark of it all.

People are so busy looking back at their past, they see no future. But if we would look back and see what God has done for us, we would see our path strewn with debris that God has lifted off us, but we would also see blessings in its place. Treasure for trash!

Don't forfeit your future because of your past. Get wisdom, the principle thing, and get knowledge. The Bible says, "*My people are destroyed for lack of knowledge...*" (Hosea 4:6 KJV) Don't self-destruct because you lack knowledge and wisdom. James said, "*If any of you lack wisdom, let him ask of God, that giveth to all men liberally, and upbraideth not; and it shall be given him. But let him ask in faith, nothing wavering. For he that wavereth is like a wave of the sea driven with the wind and tossed. For let not that man think that he shall receive any thing of the Lord. A double minded man is unstable in all his ways.*" (James 1:5-8 KJV)

Be encouraged and take your mountain. It's God's gift to you (Deuteronomy 1:21).

Caleb said the following to Joshua, "*... and now, here I am this day, eight-five years old. As yet I am as strong this day as on the day that Moses sent me; just as my strength was then, so now is my strength for war, both for going out and for coming in. Now therefore, give me this mountain of which the Lord spoke in that day; for you heard in that day how the Anakim were there, and that the cities were great and fortified. It may be that the Lord will be with me, and I shall be able to drive them out as the Lord said.*" (Joshua 14:10-12 NKJV) "*But there remained among the children of Israel seven tribes which had not yet received their inheritance. Then Joshua said to the children of Israel: "How long will you neglect to go and possess the land which the Lord God of your fathers has given you?*" (Joshua 18:2, 3 NKJV)

Here is a major problem with most believers today. They do not know what belongs to them, yet, it is all found in the Book. They just won't read it to find out what is theirs. It is one thing to cross over to your Promised Land. It is another thing to know why. "I'm here, now what Lord?" "Why am I here? Why did you bring me this far? It all looks the same." "It doesn't look much different over here then it was over there." This also happened to the Israelites. (Numbers 14:2-4). They wandered for forty years in the wilderness but at one point in time, wanted to go back to Egypt, their place of bondage and slavery. Why? They didn't know what they had been delivered from and delivered to. It's one thing to know where you came from. It is still another thing to know where you are going. People who don't know where they are going will not recognize God's blessings when they arrive. It will look exactly like what they were just delivered from (Deuteronomy 8). I've watched so many Christians, myself included, go right back to the hog pen, even though God had set life before them (Deuteronomy 30:19). It was a matter of choice.

Yes, by all means, take your mountain and do it by force if force is required. The devil is not going to relinquish his hold on your "stuff" just because you say it's yours. You must TAKE it, but you cannot do it alone. God must go before you. He must be with you. He must be your support before, during and after your journey to the top. If God does not go up with you, you will lose your battle for the top. (Deuteronomy 1:42-45) Do not go alone and do not go presumptuously thinking God will okay your works. (Deuteronomy 1:43) It could be a fatal mistake.

Give me that mountain! It's mine. If God said it's mine, then it's mine. In my first book, "Journey to the Top", I talked about The Enchanted Rock in Fredericksburg, Texas. I have climbed it several times starting in my mid sixties and the last time was in 2005, I was 74. I plan on doing it again in 2006 when I'm 75. If God said it is my mountain to climb, then I will climb it. "How long will you continue to climb it, Bill?" I'll climb until I can't climb it any more, that's how long. When I'm 100 years old, I'll rent a "chopper" (if I can't climb it) to take me to the top. Then I can help others up the mountain. "C'mon up, the view is wonderful up here!"

You cannot encourage people from the ditch. "C'mon down. It's really nice down here." No, don't invite people into the ditch and don't accept any invitations to live in a ditch. Get out of the ditch and show people how to do likewise. Get on top of your situation and show others how to do the same. Get on top of the mountain of debt surrounding you, and show others, that they too, can prevail against the fiery darts of the devil. No weapon formed against you can prosper if you are heading for the top. But in a ditch, they can hurt you. In a ditch, you have no room to fight back. But on top of your mountain, you have all the room you need to take a stand and fight back.

How long will you wait to be all that God has created you to be? Caleb was eight-five and said in so many words, "I am as strong now as I ever was. Give me that mountain. With God's help I can take it."

We need to understand that if God is for you and me, it doesn't matter who is against us. We must also understand that we can do all things through Christ who gives us the strength to cross over troubled waters. We must understand that God Himself crosses over before us and makes things ready and safe. "*The LORD thy God, he will go over before thee, and he will destroy these nations from before thee, and thou shalt possess them: and Joshua, he shall go over before thee, as the LORD hath said.*" (Deuteronomy 31:3 KJV) He does not send us empty handed to get the job done. He supplies all our needs according to His riches.

> **SUCCESS KEY: If you think you can, you can; if you think you can't, you can't. The first is a prescription for success, but the second is a prescription for failure.**

Mountains look different when you are in a ditch. Failure can cloud your vision. You can't see the mountaintop clearly; things are distorted. We see too much impossibility. From the ditch we say, "I can't." From the mountaintop we can say, "I made it." I'd rather be looking down on the ditch from my mountaintop position than looking out from the ditch. I'd rather be looking at the mountain(s) before me, whatever they are, and say, "Give me that mountain. With God's help I can make a difference." People in ditches have no desire to possess mountains. They're only hope is to survive while in the ditch. Even then, some have given in to the ditch mentality. "Well, I'm here. I might as well get used to it. I might as well make the best of it. After all, who am I?"

We will never climb any mountains until we have learned to declare war on that which is holding us back. If it is a mountain of debt that is holding you back, declare war. If your marriage is going south and your headed north, don't give up; declare war. If your business is going sour, don't give up; declare war. If lack of finances is your issue, declare war and fight back. If drug addiction is your problem, fight back. Declare war! If alcohol is holding you back, declare war. Whatever is holding you back from what God said is yours, take it by force. Fight back and declare war! If God be for you, who can be against you? No weapon formed against you shall prosper if you will take a fighting stance and declare war. "Devil, if it's war you want, its war you'll get. I'm taking back what you've stolen from me." Remember, the blood of Jesus covers it all!

The phrase "go up" is found in the Bible 134 times. The phrase "go down" is found only 81 times. Maybe God wants us to go up more times than He wants us to go down. The phrase "go over" is found 33 times, "go beyond" three times, "go to" 112 times, and the phrase "get up" three times. God is interested in us going somewhere, not hanging around waiting and keeping our fingers crossed hoping that something good will come of it all. You cannot successfully climb to greater heights in God if all you do is hang around the bottom of the mountain.

The problem with most people is that they can't climb over the rubble (their past) to even get to the foot of the mountain. That happened to me at the Enchanted Rock. There was so much fallen rock at the base of the mountain that I had to climb over or go around to even get started in my upward climb. That took almost a half hour. The thought of quitting often entered my mind, or tried to. I never let that negative thought of quitting take root in my thinking. I was going to the top no matter the rubble of my past. I was going back to Houston with a story, my story!

The problem with most people is that they just drift along with the tide, "Whatever will be, will be. Who cares? I'm just a no body, going nowhere." If you won't "take" your mountain, it will take you. The size will overwhelm you unless you whittle it down to your size and then beat the devil out of it. He is generally the culprit to blame anyway. If you're a drifter, settling for any old port, then that is exactly what you will get. If you have no solid foundation, then you will drift aimlessly and without purpose. A ship, whose anchor is not firmly attached to something solid enough to hold it in place, will drift with the tides. Where it ends up is anybody's guess. If your anchor is not the Lord, you will drift with the tides of failure, fear, rejection and turmoil. Any old port will do. Jesus is the Solid Rock. Cast your anchor (life) on Him for He can hold you in place. He can stop the tides of failure in your life and cause you to want to take your mountain, not it over take you.

In Joshua 14:10-12, he (Caleb) said that the Anakim were there and that the cities were great and fortified. "...*Nevertheless, if the Lord will be with me, I shall be able to drive them out as the Lord said.*" This statement is the key to your success.

The story of the Anakim is found in Numbers 13:16-33. Moses had sent some spies on an assignment to find out what the land was like in the southern part of the land of Canaan. They came to Hebron where descendants of a race of giants called the Anakim lived. They report back to Moses, telling him in part, that there were some giants inhabiting the land. "*We felt as small as grasshoppers, and that is how we must have looked to them.*" (Numbers 13:33)

That's the problem with most people. When a problem arises, we see it bigger than the solution within it. The spies had found some grapes, but also some giants. That's quite normal in that you will find both good and bad when heading up your mountain. There will be some ditches along the way but there will also be some great experiences. The spies had a good report but intermingled within it was some bad news. "I found the grapes but how am I going to get past those giants to get them?" "I see the mountain of debt before me but how am I going to get over that mountain and solve the problem when there are so many giants surrounding it? "God, I know you want me to be more than a conqueror, but there are so many giants! I'm beaten before I start; the cards are stacked against me. It's over before I can even get started so how can I win with so much against me?"

Deuteronomy 1:26-33 tells us more. Here was the problem; the spies murmured and complained. "God must hate us. He wants to destroy us. True, He brought us out of bondage (Egypt) but look at where we are now. We are no further ahead now then we were when we were in Egypt. Where can we go up? How can we go up? Our brethren have discouraged us. There are great cities and they are well fortified and there are giants. Why me, God?"

The spies saw at least three things that said "impossible"."There is no way. We will never be able to carry out this assignment." They saw: 1) cities that were great, 2) cities that were well fortified, and 3) giants. That's quite a combination. To the ordinary person, this would spell a triple threat. But to God's children, it is only another problem waiting to be solved. Problems are our assignments to solve so that we might get beyond the problem to our Promised Land. "Let's see. How can I turn this thing around to my advantage? How can I get control of this? What can I do to make it bow to me, not me bow to the problem and quit?"

Most people would have quit after seeing that their problem was like the "great cities" the spies had seen. "Wow, those sure are some big cities. How are we ever going to get past them to our "grapes" (blessings)?"

When I first came to Houston in 1960, I got lost more times than I can count because I was unfamiliar with Houston and its surroundings. I'd never been there before. To climb your mountain successfully, you must have direction to your stuff. Otherwise, any handout will do. You must be familiar with the Word of God or you will flounder like a fish out of water.

The second thing the spies saw was how well fortified these great cities were; now the problem doubled. And, of course, the third thing they saw was the giants themselves.

I'll never forget coming to Houston for the first time. I had been living in Dallas for about two years and decided to move to Houston. Now, I'm from the small town of Bath, in the State of Maine, right up on the northeast tip of the U.S. When I was growing up there, the population was not more than 6,000 people. There were two main streets; Front Street and Center Street. There was nothing overwhelming about Bath, then or now. I was, and am, familiar with its layout.

We move forward to the year 1960 and I am headed south on I-45 and I catch my first glimpse of Houston. It was absolutely overwhelming; it was so huge. And it was well fortified with tall buildings and freeways and everything else that would dazzle the mind of a small town boy like me. It was like an impenetrable fortress waiting to devour those not familiar with its complexity. I thought, "I could get lost in this place. How will I ever find my way around? If I get lost, how will anyone ever find me?" But rather than let it "get me", I got it, and drove into downtown Houston. The great, fortified city of Houston totally enveloped me.

Within hours from my arrival, I found a place to stay and a few days later landed a job. Over the next few weeks and months, I checked the place out. I became familiar with Houston and its surroundings. I ventured out past those areas I was familiar with and into places yet discovered. It wasn't long before I knew my way around quite well. Yes, there were a few ditches along the way but I came out of them all with God's help and I began to climb mountains.

I did not know about giants as I do now (Hosea 4:6). The Lord was not in my life. I had surrendered to the giants, not to Him. That didn't happen until April, 1976. *"That if thou shalt confess with thy mouth the Lord Jesus, and shalt believe in thine heart that God hath raised him from the dead, thou shalt be saved. For with the heart man believeth unto righteousness; and with the mouth confession is made unto salvation.* (Romans 10:9, 10 KJV)

I began to know truth and how to stay out of the ditches and climb mountains. Although I've killed a few giants along the way, I still have a way to go. There are still a few giants left out there and I'm after them. You see, in Christ, I can do all things; even kill a few more giants. I've dealt them a few blows and they have dealt me a few but greater is He that is in me then he that is in the world.

During the past 46 years I have experienced some awesome times in Houston even though I met a few giants along the way. During that time, two daughters were born. Later, they married and now I have two sons in law AND four grandchildren. I go back to my hometown in Maine once a year to visit family and eat a few lobsters but I sure like getting back to Houston.

I saw opportunity in Houston. Our spies saw great, fortified cities and giants. There was something else. They felt as small as grasshoppers but only when they saw the giants. They did a comparison, which is something we should never do. "They're so big and we're so little. How will we ever get to our Promised Land?"

They not only saw themselves as grasshoppers but the giants saw them as grasshoppers.

You will never climb out of your ditches and head for the mountaintops until you whittle the giants in your life down to your size. This also means that you must see yourself bigger than a grasshopper. You are a giant in God's eyes. Act like one! Never let a giant (problem) look down on you. You look up at it and bring it down to size. That is called "giant management".

David did that to Goliath in I Samuel 17 and all it took was a few smooth stones and a slingshot. It worked because David came in the Name of the Lord. He didn't attack his giant presumptuously or in his own power. He knew he could not win, but in God he knew all things were possible. Verse 50 tells us that David prevailed over the giant.

You, to, can prevail over your giants. Take charge! Take your mountain! It isn't over until God says it's over. In the meantime, beat up on a few giants; take them down and put them under your feet. For those of you who are not Bible smart, that is where the devil belongs; under your feet. Now go collect some "grapes". It will be well worth the effort, the time and the journey will be SUPER!

Chapter Nine

Stop Entertaining the Ghosts of Your Past Failures

"I, even I, am he that blotteth out thy transgressions for mine own sake, and will not remember thy sins. Put me in remembrance: let us plead together: declare thou, that thou mayest be justified." (Isaiah 43:25-26 KJV)

Stop entertaining those ghosts. Why? It's simple. They do not exist.

Have you ever entertained a ghost? I'm certain we all have unknowingly at one time or another. I know I have. Now I'm not talking about those ghoulish ghosts we might see in a horror movie. I'm talking about the ghosts of our past, our past sins and transgressions. He (the devil) never reminds us of what we did right, he only reminds us of what went wrong in our lives and how badly we messed up. He comes only but to steal, kill and destroy. He will lie to you, steal from you, kill and destroy you if he can (John 10:10). And he can if you let him. Jesus came so that we may have life and have it more abundantly. Even most of the Church today will remind us of how wrong, how bad and messed up we are. No denying we were messed up. I know because I was one of the messes, but God cleans up messes. He did mine in April of 1976; here we are thirty years later and He is still doing a work in me. I am a work in progress. Church, (this includes the preachers), if you have nothing good to say about me, then keep it to yourself. Don't remind me of what God Himself cannot remember (Isaiah 43:25-26 KJV).

There is an interesting word found in this Scripture. It is the word "blot". Ancient Scripture was written on one particular type of paper, among others, called Vellum. It is the one most are familiar with today and is used primarily for the making of drawings. Architectural and engineering companies, to name a few, use tons of it. The ink used in ancient days contained no acid; therefore, it did not penetrate the paper. It only laid on the surface. Today there are acids in the ink, among other things, and to erase a dimension or a word from a drawing on a sheet of Vellum is almost impossible because the acid has etched the words into the paper. You'll rub a hole through the paper before you can completely erase the error. Most of the time, a typo, error or wrong information is simply deleted and you start over again.

In order for a Scribe (secretaries in ancient times) to erase something written, all he had to do was blot it out with a sponge or cloth. Since the ink had not etched into the paper, it would completely disappear. There would be absolutely no trace of it whatsoever and the Vellum was used again and again. That is what God does to those who accept Him. He uses us for His glory after we have been cleaned up.

So it is with our sins and transgressions. There is no traceability, no evidence of them remains. We have been acquitted. *"Put me in remembrance: let us plead together: declare thou, that thou mayest be justified.* (Isaiah 43:26 KJV) The word "justified" can mean, "just as if I had never sinned". This means we have been found, "NOT GUILTY". Our sins and transgressions have been CANCELLED! In the New Testament, the blood of Jesus shed at the Cross of Calvary covers our sins and transgression and forgiveness erases the stench of our wrongdoing. We have been washed in the Blood of the Lamb. *"And from Jesus Christ, who is the faithful witness, and the first begotten of the dead, and the prince of the kings of the earth. Unto him that loved us, and washed us from our sins in his own blood, And hath made us kings and priests unto God and his Father; to him be glory and dominion for ever and ever. Amen."* (Revelations 1:5-6 KJV) Our sins and transgressions have been removed. As believers though, we are held accountable for all our actions. We will give account of what we did as Christians. Every word must and will be accounted for (Matthew 12:36-37).

Does our past exist? Sure it does. Do we have a past then based on this Scripture? Of course we do, but not our past sins and transgression. They're gone and you cannot be held accountable for them again. You cannot be tried twice for the same crime. Read Isaiah 53.

So what about these "ghosts" of our pasts? Why do we continue to dance with them? Why do we go round and round in circles with them? It's because we are being accused. Here is what we find in Revelations 12:10-11 (KJV), "*And I heard a loud voice saying in heaven, Now is come salvation, and strength, and the kingdom of our God, and the power of his Christ: for the accuser of our brethren is cast down, which accused them before our God day and night. And they overcame him by the blood of the Lamb, and by the word of their testimony; and they loved not their lives unto the death.*"

But how can you be accused of something that has been erased? It's the devil's purpose to accuse us and if we dwell on those accusations, they can keep us from knowing the truth. Truth makes us free but only if we KNOW it. Hearing a truth does not make us free. It is when we know and understand the truth that we are made free. "*And ye shall know the truth, and the truth shall make you free*" (John 8:32 KJV). The devil has come to accuse and condemn. But how can he condemn those who have been made free? The Bible tells us in Romans 8:1 (KJV), "*There is therefore now no condemnation to them which are in Christ Jesus...*"

If there be no condemnation, then what are we being condemned and accused of? Our past. The devil doesn't know where we are going but he sure knows where we came from. After all, before we were born again (John 3) you and I served the devil. And there are still a few, even in the Church today and as believers, following the devil. Make up your mind today who you will follow. John 3:18 says there are two groups of people; condemned and those not condemned. If Romans 8:1 is true, and it is, then that leaves one group, NOT CONDEMNED! If you do not know which group you belong in, you will go around in circles for the rest of your life trying to find what group you are supposed to be in. If you are in the wrong group, all you have to do is pray and ask Jesus into your heart. "Jesus, come into my heart and save me. I am a sinner. I have done wrong. Come into my heart and cleanse me from all unrighteousness. I receive you right now in Jesus name." If you prayed that prayer you are now in the right group according to 2nd Corinthians 5:17 (KJV). *"Therefore if any man be in Christ, he is a new creature: old things are passed away; behold, all things are become new."* Notice the word, "In" Christ. We must be "In" Christ, not just know about Him. That's where a lot of the church is today. They have heard about Christ but do not know Him intimately. He is not your buddy or your soul mate. He is not your "right hand man" or your party mate. He is to be your Lord and Savior. And until you are "In" Him, you are not part of Him at all.

There will be those multitudes who will tell you what group(s) you belong in. Don't listen to them! They are going around in circles just like you are.

What about past failures? Are they sin or have we just missed the mark intended to take us to success? Unless God gave you specific instructions as to what to do, what you failed at was not sin. You simply missed the mark, the bull's eye. You aimed too low. But, if He gave you specific instruction and you did not do as instructed, that is called disobedience and that is sin. When you know what to do according to the Word of God and do not do it, you have missed the mark. Now we are in trouble. Sin now must be dealt with. Here's how; put it under the Blood of Jesus! Don't sweep it under the carpet hoping it will go away. Deal with it, ask for forgiveness and move forward. Don't let it hamper your success journey.

Declare it! (Isaiah 43:26) But be careful what you declare. Words are all powerful and can order life or death. *"A man's belly shall be satisfied with the fruit of his mouth; and with the increase of his lips shall he be filled. Death and life are in the power of the tongue: and they that love it shall eat the fruit thereof."* (Proverbs 18:20-21 KJV) What then, should we declare? We should declare the truth because truth makes you free. Declare that you have been set free from the sins of your past. If you don't the devil will do his own declaring by way of accusations and intimidation. He'll whisper in your ear as he did Eve's in Genesis 3:1. He'll start the ball of guilt rolling with his accusations that you are guilty as charged. He'll remind you of everything he can to get you off track, God's track for your life. He will detour you with words that sound godly but are not. He brings up things in your past that you had forgotten. His only purpose is to defeat you by any means available. Remember, he has come to steal, kill and destroy. God has forgotten your past sins and transgression. The devil tries to remind you of what God has forgotten. Does the devil have a better memory than God? No, absolutely not! The devil is the father of lies. He has never said a true word about anything. He accuses! Do not buy into his game. Study the Word of God. *"Study to shew thyself approved unto God, a workman that needeth not to be ashamed, rightly dividing the word of truth."* (2 Timothy 2:15 KJV) Know your rights, know what is yours, and defend yourself. God has your back! Don't let the devil shame you and don't be ashamed! When you know the Word of God you can declare it back to the evil one and those ghoulish ghosts of your past; *YOU HAVE BEEN FORGIVEN!* If you can say nothing else, say, *"The Blood! It's all under the Blood."*

Success key: *"Submit yourselves therefore to God. Resist the devil, and he will flee from you."* (James 4:7 KJV) Now you are free to do God's will.

Remember, *"Be sober, be vigilant; because your adversary the devil, as a roaring lion, walketh about, seeking whom he may devour."* (1 Peter 5:8 KJV)

Resist the devil and serve God! Here is how you and I can resist the devil:

1. Submission to God – James 4:7
2. Word of your testimony – Revelation 6:9
3. Walk not after the flesh – Romans 8:5,7-8
4. Walk in the Spirit – Romans 8:6
5. Casting down imaginations – 2 Corinthians 10:5
6. Overcome by the blood of the Lamb – Revelations 12:11

Submit to God. That is a hard one for all of us but you must do it. Submit all of you, the whole of you, everything! Leave nothing for the devil. The devil has studied you to find a loophole. Don't let him find one. Stop giving the devil materials to work you over with.

What are you saying? Words can entice; words give room and can cause good or evil. Choose carefully your words. What words describe your testimony? Be careful that you give attention to God, not the devil.

Stop satisfying the deeds of the flesh. That's the devil's turf. Walk in the Spirit and you will not satisfy the desires of the flesh.

Cast down (put away from you) everything that is not of God. When ungodly thoughts come your way, and they will, cast them down. Do not entertain them. Don't make room for the devil in your thought life. Don't give him an open door to wreck havoc in your life. Read Matthew 12:43-45.

Plead the Blood of Jesus over everything! Your life, health, finances, relationships, church, work place, business; EVERYTHING!

Fight! The Bible says we are to fight. Look at Ephesians 6:14 which, and I'm paraphrasing, says we are to take a stand. When in trouble, don't run from it; stand your ground. Too many Christians are running from something that most of the time isn't even after them. Take a stance against the enemy and fight. Your life will depend on it!

Chapter Ten

Making Sound Investments

"For everyone who has will be given more, and he will have an
abundance. Whoever does not have, even what he has will be taken
from him." (Matthew 25:29 NIV)

What do the words invest, investing and investment mean to
you? As you think on this question, do several things come to mind?
Probably so. But for starters, here is what Webster says. To invest
in something means an act or process of expending resources
– especially money. Why would we invest? To achieve rewards. In
today's world we would think of money more than anything else. But
the word invest does not always pertain to money. In this chapter
we are going to look at the word invest in a completely different
light. It's not going to be about money. It could mean money but
I want to take you out of that mind set and cause you to think
deeper. This chapter, then, is about investing in people. A perfect
example of this is found in John 3:16. *"For God so loved that He gave*
His only begotten Son." The word gave could be rendered, invested.
God invested in you and me.

Let's investigate further.

Making anything other than sound investments is a gamble.
Godly investments are a sure thing; gambling is not!

Those who go around in circles, not knowing which way to turn,
will face failure everyday until they make up their minds to get off
the merry-go-rounds of life and invest in life rather than take from
life. When you stay on life's merry-go-rounds, you will see the same
scenery every time the merry-go-round makes another turn. If you
want to change the scenery, get off the merry-go-round, otherwise,
you have accepted, by choice, failure. When you stay on the merry-
go-round, you invest in failure. When you get off, you invest in
your future; it's called tomorrow! Failure is the flower that did

not blossom though it had all the right ingredients internally; it was meant to blossom and so were you. Failure is anything not turning out as expected. Success is that which turns out as expected. When you invest in failure, you get failure. The interest paid on failure is more failure. It's a merry-go-round and it goes nowhere. When you invest in success the whole world opens its doors for you. The Bible says the wealth of the sinner is laid up for the righteous. But not only that, God will pour blessings on you, such that, you will not be able to contain them. You will not find a container big enough to hold all that God can pour out on you. He wants to make an investment in you but here is the catch. He expects a return on His investment. When should we start investing? Today would be a good day to start. The dividends will bring a super tomorrow! Invest in today for great returns tomorrow. No investment today, no interest tomorrow. See how that works?

I've heard so many stories of how people invested in stocks years ago and have reaped a bountiful harvest today and will for the rest of their lives. Here is what the person says who made no investment. "If I had only invested in that stock in the 30's when I had the opportunity, I would have millions today. A few shares of stock purchased in XXX Company when I had the opportunity, would have generated millions today. I never invested and look where I am today. Look where I could have been had I invested in yesterday when the price was right." Wrong investments in life today can cause a very expensive tomorrow. It's like exercise or should I say the lack of it. (Whoops, there's that word so many of us hate). Don't invest in exercise today and pay the price for poor health tomorrow. Exercise is free. Sickness and disease is very expensive. Invest today for a marvelous tomorrow. Here is how it adds up. A little work today when you're young, for pleasure tomorrow when you're much older. But we have it in reverse. It's all about pleasure now, today, but what we fail to realize is that the hard work comes tomorrow. Your pleasure today comes from the hard work of yesterday. Your rewards come after the work has been done, not before.

Here is a Biblical account of investing. You know the story of the parable of the talents found in Matthew 25: 14-30. This parable is about money but there are several principles that can be learned from it and applied in all areas of life.

A man was about to go on a journey so he called in his slaves and entrusted possessions to them. To one was given five talents. To another two talents and to a third one talent **each to his own ability** and the man went on his journey. Upon returning from his journey, he asked each of the three men what they had done with the possessions he had entrusted to them. The one who had been given the five talents traded with them and gained five more talents. In the same manner, the one who had been given the two talents gained two more. But the man who had been given only the one talent hid it in the ground. The first man who had gained the five talents was given charge of many things. The one who had received the two talents was also put in charge of many things. In other words, not only did these two men get double for their trouble, they were given much more. The one who had hidden his one talent lost the talent he had buried. He wound up with nothing because he was afraid to take a risk. He did not climb his mountain. He did nothing with what he had been given although he had the same opportunity, as did the other two men.

Everyone in life is given opportunity, opportunity to invest one's time with value being the reward. The two men in our story who invested what was given them acted wisely, but the third did not. He did nothing with what he had been given and as a consequence lost everything.

Now this account is about investing another person's money. And certainly it is wise to invest one's money wisely, especially someone else's. Have you noticed that there are principles involved in our story? Can you see them? Can we use the same principles in other ways? Sure we can. But what other ways are there to invest? Let's investigate. Remember, if you are going to be successful you must use wisdom principles. They are all important. Begin by reading the wisdom chapters in Proverbs beginning with chapter one and following. There you will find the principles I am talking about.

Did you know that the cemetery is full of people who did nothing with their lives? They did not invest and they left early. What do I mean by that? They did not invest into the lives of others. We are not here on planet earth for ourselves; we are here for others. Ask yourself, "Would I be missed if I left today?" If you've been an addition to people's lives, yes, you sure would be missed. But what if you had invested nothing? That is why there are so many of what I call "the walking dead". They have contributed nothing (no-thing) and wonder why life is so cruel.

Most of the people in cemeteries died with their dreams unfulfilled. They were not givers; they were takers. And giving is a principle. Here is what the Bible says in Luke 6:38 (NIV), *"Give, and it will be given to you. A good measure, pressed down, shaken together and running over, will be poured into your lap. For with the measure you use, it will be measured to you."* Original (Bible) manuscripts had no punctuation marks or sentence structure. They were written as one very long sentence. Punctuation and sentence structure were added later so the Bible could be read more easily. So in our verse above we start with the word, "give". Let's do something. Let's add a period after the word, "give". That word by itself gives the whole of it for life, the sum total. Life should be one of giving and to give means one would invest. Invest what? Invest in the lives of others what God has given you. How much should I give? Invest all that it would take to fill the gaps in the lives of another person. Here is the rational of most people. "But that would leave me empty handed, wouldn't it?" No! Look at the rest of Luke 6:38 (NIV). *"...and it will be given to you. A good measure, pressed down, shaken together and running over, will be poured into your lap. For with the measure you use, it will be measured to you."* The question that most people would ask is this. What is it that will be given back to me? What does the word "It" mean in our Scripture? Here is the answer. IT is what you give away and IT is what comes back in good measure and then the Scripture goes on to tell us how the measure will be given. It comes back pressed down, shaken together and running over. IT then is what comes from the expenditure of our God-given resources. Here is a major key. The measure (amount) that is given us will be given in direct proportion to the measure in which we gave. In other words, what you give away comes back to you. It is known as the Law of Mutual Exchange. Church people know it as the Law of Reciprocity. If people gave as Scripture commands us, we would never be found "empty-handed". The Bible says this. "*Each man should give what he has decided in his heart to give, not reluctantly or under compulsion, for God loves a cheerful giver.*" (2 Corinthians 9:7 NIV) Then why do people fail so often in this command to give? Why do we hesitate to invest in the lives of others? It's because of our decisions. We see the word "decided" in our Scripture above. Most of the time our decision is based on what we have or do not have in the Coffers. It's not a heart matter. Here is another good question. What happens if we do not give? For the answer, let's look at the back side of Luke 6:38. It's the side that most people never investigate. Here is what we find. Don't give (bad measure) and we walk away with nothing. In other words, we will reap the same as we sow. Here is what Scripture says. "*Whoever sows sparingly will also reap sparingly. Whoever sows generously will also reap generously.*" (II Corinthians 9:6 NIV) Another word for sowing could be investing. Most people would automatically think money because for most, that is where our heart is. But it is not about investing money. It is about investing in other people's lives. Our problem with this is that we see it leaving our hands and going into the hands of another. Now we have nothing and they have our "stuff". That's because we are a greedy lot; greedy and selfish with only self in mind. That is being poverty minded and you will lose even what you already have. "*...I tell you that to everyone who has, more will be given, but as for the one who has nothing, even what he has will be taken away.*" (Luke 19:26 NIV)

It all begins with you and me. If I see a need, I invest in that need by giving to meet that specific need. But if I have that which would fill a need and do not give to that need, I will lose what I already have. When you do not give, things begin to break down. Things don't work right. Money seems to "slip through your fingers". And all of a sudden you have needs that seem to have come from nowhere. How do I get out of that situation? Start investing! Be known as an investor, a giver. Your needs will then be met and you will have an abundance of seed to plant in the lives of others. "*Now he who supplies seed to the sower and bread for food will also supply and increase your store of seed and will enlarge the harvest of your righteousness.*" (II Corinthians 9:10 NIV) In other words, God gave what you now have in your possession so as to fill the needs of others. You, in a sense of the word, are giving back to God what He gave to you. You become a conduit. It simply goes through the hands of others but He receives it as a gift back to Him. Why? So He can give more of what is needed. He could give directly to the person in need, but you and I are here to do His will. Giving is in "the will". If you read "the will" (Bible) you will see it is all about giving. (Read John 3:16.) Again, it is the Law of Mutual Exchange. God gives to you and me in order that we might give to others. It is called sound investing.

What should we invest in? What would be a sound investment? If you had opportunity to invest in something, what would it be? Do any ideas come to mind? Nothing? Are you drawing a blank? Okay, I'll give you the answer. Here it is in one word, *TODAY! Invest in today.* You cannot invest in yesterday; it's over with. You cannot invest in tomorrow; it hasn't come yet. But you can invest in today, which will profoundly affect your tomorrows. How many of your tomorrows?   *ALL OF THEM!*

Let's suppose I want to plant a garden. I've decided I want to grow some carrots, so I buy some carrot seeds. So far, so good. I have a small plot of land that looks like it might have some good soil. I've never planted a garden before. I mean, after all, how hard can that be? A few seeds, some good soil and away I go. I'm going to have some carrots! But I do nothing with the seeds. I don't plant them. There they are in their little envelopes doing nothing but waiting on me to plant them. And guess what? I have no carrots. Where are my carrots? They are in the seeds, but I must plant them in order to get my harvest. I was waiting on my harvest but I had invested nothing (no-thing) for the harvest. I walked by those little packages of seeds every day saying, "I'll get to you tomorrow. Right now I have more important things to do than investing in planting a few carrot seeds today for the harvest in my future."

Here is how most people invest in today. "I'll buy a lottery ticket. If I win, I'm good to go, I'm set. I've got it made. I can take off from life." Here is another rational. "I sure hope today is better than yesterday. It sure was a bummer." Well, of course it was. You invested nothing for a better tomorrow. You see, your success for tomorrow depends on the investment you make today. No investment today, no success tomorrow. And your investment must be more than just getting up and going to work. *You must invest in you!* One guy said, "I'm praying and keeping my fingers crossed that it will all work out. Maybe Lady Luck will shine on me. If nothing works, I'll just throw in the towel. What else is a person to do?" Praying, crossing your fingers, and luck have nothing to do with your future if all you do is mouth a few empty words thinking it will get you by. You've planted nothing. How can you expect a harvest? All you will get is more of what you had yesterday. Nothing will change until you change, and the change begins on the inside. Lady Luck (if there were such a person) can't help you. Crossing your fingers, well, that won't help either. You can change all you want on the outside but until you change on the inside, nothing much is going to happen. You'll spend a lot of money fixing up the outside while the inside goes to pot (A little pot pun there). What do you need to cross the finish line? God! He is the power you will need for the race called life. How you finish depends wholly on how much of Him you allowed in your life. If you want to finish ahead of the crowd, let God spur you forward. Not much else will work. I know. I've tried.

I have known others who, when depressed, bought a newer toy, bigger and shinier, as an investment for happiness. After the newness wore off it was back to square one. Why? The investment was external to satisfy the internal. Godly investments produce God results. We are made in His image and likeness (Genesis 1:26) so work must be done on the image (not self image). Work on the God image and the self image will come around. If you want to improve the self image get the God image right. We need to start today to be like Him.

What then, do I have to work with? For starters, you've been given life. What will you do with it? You've been given time, 24 hours a day. All of us have an equal amount of time. What will you do with those hours? How will you best use them? We've been given all we need to be prosperous and have great success. How we use what we have been given determines our outcome. What do you see when you look backwards in your life, weeds or flowers?

Follow the directions. When the directions say don't turn here, DON'T; and when it says turn here, DO. (Joshua 1:1-8)

The best investment you can make is in you, but you must invest in the total man; spirit, soul and body. You cannot leave any of these three out. You must attend them all. Feed each one or starve them all. A starved spirit is of no value to any one unless it is starving for truth. Starving any of these three areas is to stunt their growth. You will walk lopsided. It is God who sets us apart whole-ly. To be made whole is to "feed" constantly and consistently the whole of man. It is a wise investment! Unfortunately, we follow trends and millions are building up the body but starving the soul and spirit thinking it solves life's problems. Not so! They're not whole! Yes, it is good to build the body and keep it healthy but not at the expense of starving those significant others, the soul and spirit. What good is a great looking body if the soul and spirit are crying out, "Feed me, feed me," and you do not?

Here is one "proof" text as to the trinity of man for those "Doubting Thomas" individuals. *"And the very God of peace sanctify you wholly; and I pray God your whole **spirit and soul and body** be preserved blameless unto the coming of our Lord Jesus Christ."* (I Thessalonians 5:23 KJV)

Which should we invest in first? Our Scripture above gives the answer and order. Its spirit, soul and body. Now remember that the body is important because it is the temple. It houses our spirit and soul. It also is the dwelling place of the Holy Spirit at rebirth. (John 3:1-8) Here it is in I Corinthians 6:19 (KJV). *"What? Know ye not that your body is the temple of the Holy Ghost which is in you, which ye have of God, and ye are not your own?"* No one wants to live in a messy house, especially the Holy Spirit. The spirit of man is the real person. It is not the body. The body is the house. The soul of man is the seat of our will, emotions and decision-making. A healthy body carries a healthy soul and spirit. When all three are "built up", you have a well-rounded person and happy person. More on this in my upcoming book, "Adventures in Healthy Living". For now, I think you get the idea. Meanwhile, invest in the whole of you for a better tomorrow.

Investing in today brings great tomorrows. Invest in today, today! Jesus did in Mark 1:35 (KJV), *"And in the morning, rising up a* great while before day, he went out, and departed into a solitary place, and there prayed." In Psalm 5:3 (KJV) David wrote, "My voice shalt thou hear in the morning, O LORD; in the morning will I direct my prayer unto thee, and will look up." When is a good time for preparation? In the morning! It will dictate the rest of the day.

Investing is preparedness. You prepare for failure or success. Preparation takes place today for your success tomorrow. What are you preparing for, failure or success? The words prepare and prepared are found 197 times in the Bible. Apparently, preparation is a very good thing. When should we prepare? The phrase, "In the morning" is found 96 times in the Old Testament and twelve times in the New Testament. I would say that investing and preparation could almost be used interchangeably. Investing is preparation for my tomorrows. Whether it is failure or success, I will receive a harvest tomorrow based on what I planted today. Some of us might want to pray for crop failure right now because of what we just planted!

Go ahead, invest in you; you're worth it! God sacrificed His Son to show you how much He cares for you. Order your day beginning in the morning. You will be surprised at how well it will turn out. Don't let the devil get a jump-start on you. It will ruin your day.

Chapter Eleven

Digging Your Way Out

It seems to me that those who are digging in the wrong direction are the ones who are failing all the time. Assuming you are in a ditch, as most of us are or will be, at some point in our lives, we're supposed to be digging ourselves out, not deeper. That's called, futility! If you're going to dig, use the shovel called wisdom and dig up, not down. There is a way out and it is not down. It is UP! Dr. B

If you're in a ditch, at least get up as far as your knees; from that position of surrender, you can at least look up and see God. He is your way out of your ditch. Remember that no ditch is so deep that God cannot find you.

A ditch is nothing more than a void. It is an empty place waiting to be filled in. Fill it in with the Word of God. When and if you should fail and fall, you will fall back on the Word of God. It will save your day!

Life is all about living above my circumstances. When I am gone, for what will I be best known? The number of times I was in a ditch, or the number of times I got out of them, or the times I could have made it out of the ditch and did not. 1931 – 0000. Those are the dates that will be on my tombstone. The dash represents my life here on earth. For what will I be remembered? Will people walk by and say, "He was always in some kind of a ditch (trouble)." Or will they say, "He really made something of himself. He was always trying to help others out of the ditches of life."

You cannot influence any one from a ditch. "Hey, c'mon down. It's great here in this ditch." Here is how it should go. "Hey, you down there in the ditch, c'mon up here. It's really great! Let me show you how to live life!"

I got in quite a few ditches in my younger years. The trouble was I did not know I was in a ditch. I got into the ditch of alcoholism. Then there was the ditch of failed relationships (plural). On top of that were the ditches of negative thinking. That was a super deep one for me. Then there was the ditch of religion. That was a really hard one. It took years to get out of that ditch. And the list is endless. I lived most of my early life in ditches. That is NOT the way to live nor is it the way God intended you and me to live. Jesus said that He has come to give us life and life more abundantly (John 10:10). It doesn't sound to me like ditches are the way to live. How about you? It's a choice but one I hope you will not make. Why would you, when the abundant life is available? Why live under a bridge when you could be headed for a mansion?

Don't you just hate it when you have to dig yourself out from under a mess, especially when it is a mess you have made? I do. The Bible says (paraphrased from Proverbs 26:27), "You've made your bed, now lie in it." Here it is from the KJV of the Bible: "*Whoso diggeth a pit shall fall therein: and he that rolleth a stone, it will return upon him.*"

The year 2005 was a year in which many people had to dig themselves out from under the messes that hurricanes Katrina and Rita left. Nine-eleven in NYC was another of those times; people literally digging people out from under debris. But those are not the messes I want to talk about. I want to talk about the messes we make ourselves; messes sometimes so deep that it would seem impossible to ever dig ourselves out, but somehow we do; not all, but some. Others stay buried forever in their own messes. You've often heard people say, "What a mess this is" or, "What a mess you've got yourself into this time" or, "I've never seen such a mess. Why did you do that?" We generally say this to a youngster who has been outside playing in the mud or whatever else has gotten him or her dirty. I've heard others say, "What a mess you are," or, "You sure are a mess. Come here, let me clean you up." God said that to me when I asked Him into my life. "Come here, Bill. You sure are a mess but I think I can do something with you. Let me clean you up and see what lies underneath all this mess." And so He started the cleaning process. It was okay until He got to scrubbing real hard and sort of took some hide with it. He's not through with me yet. I have a little way to go. I have some places that need extra cleaning solution to get all the spots, wrinkles and blemishes out. It might take awhile, but hey, it will be worth it. That cleaning solution is called His Blood because His Blood covers it all and from that Blood comes the love, grace, mercy and some more love and forgiveness just to mention a few of the things God has in His cleaning kit. You've no doubt heard this before. P.B.P.W.M.G.I.N.F.W .M.Y., which means, "Please be patient with me, God is not finished with me yet."

For lack of a better term, I call these messes "ditches". Ditches are where the discards are. They are the places where people throw away what they don't want any longer. They're places for run-off after a storm. They are the gathering places for what's leftover after the storm passes. It's where we drop off our "stuff", which sometimes includes relationships, when we have no more use of them.

There are all kinds of "ditches". There can be spiritual ditches, financial, relational, religious, mental, the work place, sexual, the church, marriage, the kids and business ditches to name only a few. There is a myriad of them. There are enough to go around more than once. You'll never run out of ditches should you choose to live in one or more of them. Some people that I have known over the years were living in more than one ditch at a time. Some marriages are like that. You can have a marriage going south because of finances or the lack there of, sexual problems, kid problems, the work place problems, employer/employee problems and coming at you all at once at break-neck speed; you are overwhelmed and want to go hide. It's nearly impossible to dig yourself out of those kinds of messes, at least by yourself. Key word: NEARLY impossible; which means there is hope and that hope is found only in Christ.

Now this is where God steps into the picture. But know this; He will not step in unless He is invited. You can lay in the debris and stench of the ditch for as long as you want. It isn't that God doesn't care. It is because of the choices we have made. Poor choices and bad decisions can result in some ditch time. How long you want to stay in the ditch is your choice. I personally know of some people who have lived in the same ditch for 30-40 years. They will never come out because they do not know they are in a ditch.

I didn't find out about the ditches I was living in until much later in life. After some serious study and soul searching I made a choice to get out and start climbing the mountains (God's assignments) to get a better view of what was going on around me. Now I help others up out of the ditches and start them on their climb upward. That's generally how that works. God gets you out so that you can help others out. It's called the Law of Mutual Exchange.

Most people do not fight when they are in a ditch. They are too overwhelmed. Complain, yes, but not fight. Complaining only digs the ditch deeper and wider. Soon, it is too deep and too wide to get out. They just lie down and submit to that way of life. But when you make a trench out of your ditches, that's when the fighting begins.

In WWI and WWII (I wasn't there in WWI. I'm old but not that old) the ground troops dug in. By that I mean they dug not only foxholes but also trenches. Many times the trenches were the places of operations. Troops fought in them, lived in them, slept in them and ate in them, but the trench was more than that. It was a place of "digging in". It was sometimes the place of a last stand. "We fight here or die here. We will win here or die trying." It was the last resort, the point of no return. "We will not surrender. It's all or nothing, this is it."

One problem with getting out of a ditch (situation) is that we try to do it all ourselves. "I did it, God. I got out. A little 'atta boy' would be great right about now." The problem is this; God gets no glory. By the time we dig ourselves out, we are too tired to fight the good fight of faith and we collapse. With God's help we would have been so much better off.

Hear me child of God. The devil knows when you are in a ditch. You are covered up with your own mess. He thinks you can't extricate yourself. He thinks he has you where he wants you, unable to fend for yourself. But when you make a trench out of your ditches, digging in for a final stand saying, "Enough is enough, devil. You ain't getting any more of me. I'm coming out. My back might be up against the wall but I am not quitting. I'm not taking anymore." That's when you will come out of your ditch. The devil is a liar. He can't keep you in a ditch. Plead the Blood of Jesus over your situation. The devil hates the Blood because there is Power in the Blood. Nothing can prevail over the Blood. When the devil sees your intention of coming out of the ditches, he'll leave and in a hurry. But he's a sucker for punishment; he'll be back for a more opportune time, especially when he thinks he might get another shot at you. Luke 4:13 (KJV) says this, "*And when the devil had ended all the temptation, he departed from him for a season.*"

Winners win; losers lose. Don't give the devil another shot at you. Keep moving; he can't hit a moving target.

The title of the first chapter in this book is "Get off Your Merry-go-round and Head for the Top". Have you noticed it has the word *merry* in it? Merry means to be full of fun and laughter, lively and cheerful, doing that which is conducive to fun. It means to be festive and be full of gaiety. It can last for a short time, a day or two or for a long time. Generally, for kids, it is short lived. While they are on the merry-go-round, they are having fun. When they get off, the fun stops and they want to go on another ride to continue the fun time they are having.

Many people are like that. They're having fun for all the wrong reasons and doing nothing but going around in circles. Once they recognize the futility of it all, they get off the merry-go-round and for a time seem to be headed the right direction. But then another opportunity comes along. At least they think it is an opportunity, but it is a trick, a disguise from the devil to get them back on the merry-go-round, going nowhere. If you're going nowhere, he has you where he wants you. When that supposed opportunity comes along, the unsuspecting person hops back onto the merry-go-round for another non-productive ride oblivious to the fact they ain't goin' nowhere. They have been duped; its ditch time again! And the more you wind up in the ditches of life, the harder it becomes to dig yourself out.

If you're not having any fun while on your merry-go-round ride, then something is wrong. Many people try to have fun while they are in a ditch oblivious to the dangers there. "Okay, so I am an alcoholic but I sure am having fun," as they stagger through life's stages oblivious to the dangers hidden behind every drink. It's called delusion. "Okay, so I'm in an abusive relationship, but he loves me. I just know it will work out some day so I'll just grin and bear it until he changes." Here is another case of futility. "Someday things will get better. There is nothing I can do about my situation right now. I'll just put up with it. It's bound to get better; it sure can't get any worse." They're living in denial and that is not a river in Egypt. There is a mess to be cleaned up, but for the time being let's just have some fun and forget the mess. Messes can be serious stuff. Ditches can be serious.

Have you ever been in a ditch and got stuck there seeing no immediate way out of your dilemma? I have a few times; one of which I remember quite well.

I had been on an old logging road, many of which can be found in my home State of Maine. That's where I was raised the first seventeen years of my life. I still like to explore those old logging roads, sometimes traveling on a four-wheeler several miles into the backwoods of Maine. It's fun as long as you don't get lost; and you can if you're not careful. But on this particular day it was freezing cold. You see it was winter in Maine and you do not want to get caught in the backwoods in the winter. I was in my old '39 Dodge (what's that?) moving at the breakneck speed of about 3 or 4 miles per hour. It was near dark which means it was about 4:00 PM. Rounding a bend in the old slab wood road, I tried to miss a ditch. It didn't look like much and I thought, "Well if I miss it okay, if I don't, okay. I can get myself out. I've got chains and whatever else I might need to get out of any dilemma I might get myself into." There was snow all around. I made it through the ditch okay except for the right rear wheel. It went into the ditch. "No big deal! Rocking the car from reverse to forward takes some dexterity, but I'll get out in a minute as I get some momentum moving backward and forward." All I was doing was digging my self deeper; the constant spinning of that back wheel, because of friction and heat, was melting the ice and snow making mud, slush and slop. The next thing I knew, I was stuck big time. Getting out of my car, I surveyed the damage. "I'll just jack that wheel up, put some branches under it or whatever else I can find that will give me some traction, and simply drive out of the ditch." I did all that and it didn't work. I was still stuck. I got back in my car to try and figure a way out of this problem. Nothing immediate came to mind. I was too cold to think. Something happens to the brain when it is twenty below zero, at least it does mine. I was drawing nothing but blanks. I could hear my mother's voice, "Well, William, this is another fine mess you've got yourself into." It was around 7:00 p.m. now and everything around me was freezing, including the slush in the ditch where that back wheel rested. The ditch had now become a frozen mass of ice. I was going nowhere, at least not right away. It was pitch black now and I had no light. There was only one thing to do; wait until the next light which would be in the morning, and walk to my sister's house which was a couple of miles away. This walk included a stroll across a frozen pond. It was quite breezy as I recall. Downright cold would be a better way of putting it!

In the morning I made the walk to my sister's in the freezing cold. She was just getting up and asked a silly question, "What brings you here, William, so early in the morning?" As I was telling my story, embarrassingly so, my brother-in-law, Clarence, came in. "Okay, William, let's get you out of this mess you've got yourself into." We drove to the scene of my embarrassment, broke away the ice now surrounding that back wheel, hooked a chain onto my bumper and to the back of Clarence's car which he had situated on some solid ground, and out came the stuck auto. Clarence went on his way, and I, mine.

Getting home with ice-caked chains in hand, I entered the inner sanctum of my house where Mother was waiting. I had been gone all night and had forgotten my cell phone, otherwise, I would have called her to let her know I was only stuck in my own mess for a short time and would be home momentarily. Well, it could have happened that way except it was in the early 40's; 1940's that is.

I didn't have a "merry" time stuck in that ditch. It was my own mess. I should have watched my time more carefully. I was having fun just driving around in those backwoods without a care in the world, but in trying to dig myself out of the ditch, I actually dug myself deeper. Spinning your wheels isn't something you do when you're stuck in ice and snow. The friction, in case you haven't figured it out, causes the ice to melt, but it was so cold the slush quickly became a mass of ice again. I should have put the chains on first and then eased myself out of the ditch.

I said earlier that my brother-in-law, Clarence, had situated his car on some solid ground. It actually was an outcropping of rock just big enough to get his cars rear wheels on for great traction.

Let's talk for a minute about the solid ground, or, as the Bible calls it, Solid Rock. Do you remember this old hymn? *"On Christ the solid Rock I stand, all other ground is sinking sand. All other ground is sinking sand."* If you are not on the Solid Rock or Foundation, all else will fail.

Here are two Scriptures that come to mind regarding the Rock (Jesus) who is our foundation. Upon Him, all else is built. *"Therefore whosoever heareth these sayings of mine, and doeth them, I will liken him unto a wise man, which built his house upon a rock: And the rain descended, and the floods came, and the winds blew, and beat upon that house; and it fell not: for it was founded upon a rock. And every one that heareth these sayings of mine, and doeth them not, shall be likened unto a foolish man, which built his house upon the sand: And the rain descended, and the floods came, and the winds blew, and beat upon that house; and it fell: and great was the fall of it. And it came to pass, when Jesus had ended these sayings, the people were astonished at his doctrine."* (Matthew 7:24-28 KJV)

I Corinthians 10:4 (KJV) says this, *"And did all drink the same spiritual drink: for they drank of that spiritual Rock that followed them: and that Rock was Christ."*

If Clarence had positioned his car on something other than that outcropping of rock, he would never have been able to pull me out of the ditch because he would have had no solid footing or foundation. He had the power, which was his automobile, but power is useless if you are in sinking sand. When you apply the power, you simply sink deeper into your dilemma. I, too, had the power (my car) when I was in my "stuck" place. The one thing missing was the solid ground. I could not get out by myself. I needed help.

That's the picture we get of people today trying to get out of trouble. They make two mistakes; 1) they are trying to do it all in their own power, and 2), they have no solid footing or foundation from which to extricate themselves from the grip of failure. If you were to interview the average John and Jane Doe, you would find that most of them do not want to be held in the grip of drugs, alcoholism, sexual sin, failing marriages and relationships or anything else that keeps them bound up. People want their freedom. Even an animal gets tired of being tied up all the time. Drugs and alcohol are very serious problems as are all the other problems that keep us separated from God and what He has to offer us. I know; I've been through most of those problems. Notice, I said, THROUGH. Those problems do not control me any more. I control them through the Word of God and the Holy Spirit who gives me the guidance I need to stay on the "straight and narrow". Would you believe that even as a young kid, I had had a serious drug problem? I know you do not believe me, but I did! My mother "drug" me to church, drug me to the prayer meetings and even drug me to a few funerals that, in those years, were held in the houses of the deceased. Thank God, she "drug" me to those things. I remember them to this day, some 70 years later. She knew where I would have been headed had she not "drug" me to church. It sure paid great dividends.

There are several ways in which you can wind up in a ditch.

Careless Words - There are a lot of people who have talked themselves into a few ditches in their lives. Disobedience to God's instructions could land you in a ditch for a time until you have learned the valuable lesson He is trying to teach you. Ditch time is not always all bad; it can be a learning experience. If this is your case, settle down and learn. Fussing about your dilemma will only cause you to sink deeper into your ditch situation. Trying to dig your way out when God wants you to spend more time in the "ditch of learning" can also prove futile. The "ditch of learning" can be likened unto the potter's wheel. If what you are making doesn't turn out right the first time, you start again and again until you have it right. That is what God does with His children. Generally speaking, that is accomplished in the ditches. *"And the vessel that he made of clay was marred in the hand of the potter: so he made it again another vessel, as seemed good to the potter to make it."* (Jeremiah 18:4 KJV) Self-fulfilling prophecy can land you in the ditch. "God ain't ever done anything for me, so why should I try? After all, who am I that He should notice me?" "Okay (God speaking) let's get in

some ditch time. You need it. It's the only place I can teach you."
It's sort of like the visits I had to the woodshed with my mother.
Disobedience brought swift punishment. Whining and complaining
will have its rewards too; we call it "ditch time". We could also call
those ditch times, wilderness times. It may take awhile to get to
your destination if all you do is complain about what life has handed
you. Maybe you brought most of it on yourself. After all, you could
have said no to that temptation, but instead you listened to a wrong
voice and look where you are now.

One major problem, as I see it, is that most people are listening
to wrong voices. Those voices are misleading and we wind up in
worse trouble. We seek help from wrong sources hoping they have
our answers to getting out of the ditch. "Dig here, this is the way
out," one voice says. "No, dig over here. This is a sure-fire method
for getting out of ditches," another voice says.

Look at Matthew 7:24 (KJV) again, *"Therefore whosoever heareth
these sayings of mine, and doeth them, I will liken him unto a wise man..."*
Notice the words, "Sayings of mine." It does not say listen to the
wisdom of the world. It says to listen to what God has to say.
This Scripture implies two things, hearing and doing. This, however,
is predicated on hearing right things, isn't it? In other words, be
certain you are hearing right things from right sources. This is what
keeps us out of the ditches. You've got to first *hear* right things in
order to *do* right things. You cannot rely on just any voice. It has to
be the right voice or you will find yourself in a ditch; ditches (plural)
if you live long enough. Here are more Scriptures that reinforce
what I have been saying. They all have to do with *hearing* and *doing*.
A hearing person is one who is listening for proper instruction
(guidance) which will give direction to Godly destination(s), which
by the way, is not to lead you in a ditch.

- Observe to do according to all the law (which means get proper instruction before embarking on your journey, wherever that might be).

- Do not turn from it to the right hand or the left (proper direction from right voices will keep you on the right path).

- Be hearers and doers of the Word. The Word (Bible) is your direction for missing life's ditches. You may hit a few but you will miss most of them. The number of ditches you find yourself in will depend mostly on how well you listened and followed instructions.

- A wise man will hear and increase. Are you increasing or decreasing?

- My son, hear my instruction (wisdom calling); be a listener. Most people are talking too much; giving bad direction that causes most people to do some ditch time.

- Walk not in the counsel of the ungodly (wrong voices).

- Fools despise wisdom and instruction. In other words, don't listen to fools who are going nowhere. If they are going nowhere, why would you want to go with them?

- Incline your ear to wisdom. When wisdom speaks, get close enough to hear what she is saying and then do it.

- Discretion will preserve you; understanding will keep you. Separate the chaff from the wheat; the weeds from the flowers. *"My sheep hear my voice, and I know them, and they follow me:"* (John 10:27 KJV) The key words here are, MY VOICE. His words (direction) are what you need to get out of the ditches. Start digging in the Word of God to find direction for your life. The only way out is UP!

These and many more are words of wisdom found in the Bible. Read it daily. There is no sense in spending most of your life in a ditch. You can't help any one while living in a ditch, not even yourself.

Wrong voices will keep us in the ditch. They will keep us going around in circles. They will keep us forever trying to dig our way out of our messes to no avail. Ditches have no solid footing or foundation from which to stand on and get us out of the ditches.

Here is a biblical example of listening to wrong voices. God gave Adam instructions (good voice) as to what he could and could not eat (all trees except the tree of the knowledge of good and evil) in the garden found in Genesis 2:16-17. Eve comes on the scene in Genesis 2:21-22. The serpent comes along and gives Eve an earful in Genesis 3:1 (wrong voice).

Eve listens to the wrong voice and gets her husband involved in the plot that the serpent has set up for both of them (and you and I). This scene, which I am paraphrasing, takes place in Genesis 3:6-13. God comes along with an interesting question. He asks, "Where are you, Adam?" Adam answers, "I'm over here in this ditch, God." God responds, "Have you messed up, Adam?" "Yep, sure have and that woman you gave me made me do it. She is to blame." Then God asks Eve a question. "What is this you have done?" Eve answers the question with, "The devil made me do it." AND WE HAVE BEEN IN A DITCH EVER SINCE! It is all because someone listened to a wrong voice.

It's good to ask questions. God did of Adam. Notice He asked Adam the question first, not Eve (Genesis 3:9). A man should be responsible for his actions. "Why are you in the ditch, Adam? Is there any reason for this?" Of course, Adam tried to get out of the ditch the wrong way. He dug himself deeper by trying to evade the question. Eve did the same thing.

There are a few questions we should ask ourselves but first things first. We must recognize that we are in a ditch. Of course, the one we should address our questions to should be the Lord. Man won't tell you the truth. God will.

- ➢ Why am I here in this ditch?
- ➢ How did I get here?
- ➢ Where did I go wrong?
- ➢ What can I do to get out?
- ➢ What must I do to get out?
- ➢ What life lesson is there to be learned?
- ➢ How can I apply it?

There are a few more things. Forgiveness! It is absolutely crucial that you forgive yourself AND forgive others. Otherwise, you stay in the ditch.

When God gives you directions as to how to get out of the ditches of life, don't ask questions. Don't keep digging in the wrong direction. This is not the time to question God (or any other time for that matter). Do as He says; get out and stand up straight, knowing that God has delivered you from the "pit". "Yeah, but what if it doesn't work?" No, it WILL work! Just do it! "Do you want out of the ditch?" "Yes, I do". Then do what He says do. Start digging up!

We are supposed to be salt and light according to Matthew 5:13-16. This is not accomplished while in a ditch. No one is going to come by, see you in a ditch, and think of you as salt and light. *"Let your light so shine before men, that they may see your good works and glorify your Father in heaven."* (Matthew 5:16 NKJV)

Enough about the ditches already, let's move on. I think you get the idea.

"Father in Heaven, help us to be salt and light before all of mankind that they might come to know you. In Jesus name, Amen!"

Chapter Twelve

Border Control

Yep, you heard me right partner, Border Control. I'm sure you have it confused with Border Patrol, which we have here in Texas. Among other things, the Texas Border Patrol controls the border between Mexico and Texas. They have the authority to say who comes and who goes.

God's border patrol, which is His Word, keeps us from going around in circles. We learn from His Word how to stay within His set limits, parameters and perimeters, thus keeping us out of the many ditches of life. The best thing about this is that we can still have fun. His parameters are not to keep us "hog tied" and away from any fun. No, they are designed in such a way that we can have godly fun, not godless fun.

One of the reasons we (we includes the Church) are in such a mess and continue to go around and around on our merry-go-rounds, whatever that means to you, is because we refuse to stay within the borders (perimeters) God has assigned us. I can hear some of you saying, "I didn't know He had set up borders or certain perimeters." Well, He has and He is very strict in the reinforcing of them. When He says no, He means no. We ignore the obvious signs like, no trespassing, do not enter, no admittance, and STAY OUT! When we as Christians venture out into the world, becoming a part of it, we are in no man's land and trouble will surround us. We live in the world but are to not be a part of it. We are to be separate, otherwise how will the church be recognized as the church (A called out assembly) and not as the world (See 2 Corinthians. 6:17 and Jude 1:19) The only reason we are to go out into all the world is to make disciples, not friends with the world. (See Matthew 28:19)

God knows where we can get hurt, which is why He sets up certain perimeters and parameters and expects us to adhere to what He knows is best for us.

We are testy people. We like to test God's borders, His parameters and perimeters. We like to see how far we can go without getting into serious trouble. Does God ever patrol the borders He has set up for us, and if so, how often? Does He run in shifts, such that, I might squeeze in under the fence when He isn't looking or during shift change, and go into that forbidden territory, returning before the next shift returns and before I get caught? Does He have any helpers that might squeal on us if we venture too far out of line? "Hey God," says an angel, "He's doing it again." The trespasser says, "Man, I've been caught again. You just can't get away with anything now days."

We play cat-and-mouse with God, hoping He will not catch us in a weak moment; a little closing of the eye or a little slumber. Last night while you and I slept, God was fully awake and watching ever so carefully so as to keep everything He had created in order. NOTHING escapes the eye of God. I repeat NOTHING!

Here are some interesting thoughts worth pondering. Do we enjoy sin so much that we are willing to cross the lines in spite of what could be some very serious punishment? Will the pleasure received in the crossing of the no-trespassing zones, outweigh the consequences?

In our crossing over of God's borders, we give little thought, if any, to the consequences as being severe enough to keep us from crossing over. After all, I'm a big boy now. I haven't been *whupped* in a long time." Well, get ready for a whuppin', God style, if you've crossed over His lines. And brother, He can do it! Maybe that's the problem with a lot of kids today; there is not enough parental guidance to keep them in line. When my mother gave orders to do or not do a thing, she meant business. It was that or the woodshed. Maybe a few visits to the woodshed would set matters straight with our kids today. If that doesn't work, maybe a good sound God whuppin' would get it right.

Here is what I mean by border control. My daughter, Karen, and her family and I had just returned to their house from having lunch. Kody, my eleven-year-old grandson, wanted to visit some neighbor's kids. His Mom gave him permission with certain parameters and off he went. Kory, Kody's brother, who was almost five at the time, saw an opening and asked if he could also stay outside to play. He, too, was given permission and, again, within certain parameters. His mother, (my daughter, Karen), getting down to eye level with Kory, explained those parameters. "Kory, do you understand where you can and cannot play?" "Yes, I do," was his reply, "I know I can't go out into the street." "Okay, where else can you not go?" A long hesitation meant he wasn't sure where those parameters were so Mom, again, explains. "See that line over there (pointing to her left)? That is where your yard ends. See that line over there (pointing to her right)? That is where your yard ends. You cannot cross the sidewalk because that will mean you will be on the road and we know you cannot go there." Kory shakes his head up and down meaning, "I got it, Mom. Let's move on to the good part, like, when can I go see my friends?" Mom continues with the instructions. (Instructions give guidelines in two directions; where we can go and where we cannot go. Listen carefully to instructions given. After receiving those instructions, as adults, we are free to choose our own direction.) "You cannot go in the back yard, Kory, where the swimming pool is. There has to be an adult with you." "Okay, I got it," said Kory. Then he gave a thumbs-up; he had it all under control. While Karen was giving him directions as to where his yard was, he was already within a couple of feet of his neighbor's yard. Stepping a little closer to that imaginary line, he said, "Am I still in my yard?" "Yep, you sure are, Kory. Good Boy!" He takes another small step for boy-kind getting ever so close to that line; that place of no return. If he can just cross over he will have it made. "Am I still in my yard?" "Yes, Kory, but you are getting close to where I told you, you cannot go. Be careful." He takes another step. Now he has one foot in the neighbor's yard and the other is in his yard. "Mom, am I still in my yard?" "Kory Jacob Capps, come here. We need to talk." More instructions are given to assure him of the fact that the punishment for crossing over the line will be much more severe than the pleasure of going where he was told not to go. His plan, for the moment, was put on hold. Kory thought, "Aw man, if I could have taken just one more step I would have been in my neighbor's yard having fun with my friends; maybe next time. I need more time to think this one out. There is bound to be a better way. I just gotta find a way to outsmart my Mom." Had he made it to his neighbor's yard he would have thought he had won and that Mom, since he was already in the neighbor's yard, would give in and let him stay.

Isn't that the way we are sometimes? "If I can just out smart God; I can be over the fence in a jiffy enjoying life." "If I can just get Him to "give in", I'll be home free." Nope, that dog won't hunt either, as we say in Texas. God does not give in to our demands to have it our way. God is too loving to let us have our way and destroy ourselves.

It's kind of like having your pet on one of those wind up leashes, that when let out to its maximum length, stops the animal short of its intended goal. God has to keep us on a leash, which allows us to go only so far. Yes, we can go farther, but when we do that, we are out from under the protection of God since we have decided to have it our way. The only protection we have is to be found under the wings of the Almighty.

It isn't that God doesn't want us to have fun. He simply wants us to stay in our own backyard where He can supervise us. You remember how it was without His supervision, don't you? I do. I was always in someone else's' back yard and got into trouble for it. I simply was where I was not supposed to be. My daughter Karen did this with her two boys when they were little guys. "When outside you cannot play anywhere that I cannot see you, every minute, okay?" Yes, God wants us to have fun. Think about it. How much more fun could we have had if we had stayed within those parameters God gave us which are found in His Word and not strayed over in someone else's territory? We've been given so much, why would we stray to other places? We couldn't possibly explore all that God has given us in our lifetime; it is so much. But staying in our own backyard gives us the time to explore His goodness. Here is a super success key. The grass is not greener on the other side of the fence.

The words "border" and "borders" appear 200 times in the Bible. Of course, not all pertain to physical land borders; some pertain to the border of a garment, but it is interesting that God thought about borders.

My mother thought of them too. She pointed out more places I could not go versus those places I could go. I thought that was kind of mean but as I reflect on those directions today I can see they were for my own good. I did, from time to time, trespass into those forbidden areas and, of course, got into trouble when caught red-handed. I got away with a few things, not many, but the key is that there would be consequences to reckon with sooner or later.

Here are a few borders, perimeters if you will, from the book of Proverbs. You might not see them that way but bear with me for a moment. Perimeters, borders and parameters all have "like" definitions in that they spell out places we can go and places we should not go. They are like safety zones. We find these zones in many sports arenas. If you do a certain thing, you are out of bounds and it could cost you and your team points and penalties. Proverbs 1:15 (NKJV) says this, "*My son, do not walk in the way with them,...*" What does this mean? It means we are to not flirt with evil by hanging out with the wrong crowd. In other words, don't give the devil more room to operate in your life by crossing the "borders" set up by God. The devil already has too much room and we gave it to him. If we cross the borders set up by God and "hang out" with wrong people, we get in trouble and sometimes it is very difficult to cross back into the territory assigned us. We all have border assignments. They are set up specifically for you and me and tailor made to fit each one of us. Why? Because God knows the places we should be and should not be for our own sake and safety. In many places in the Bible we are instructed to not depart from God's laws. When we do, we are in what I call a "no fly zone". We'll get "shot down" if we do. Danger signs should go up all around you. The spiritual red lights, horns, whistles and the like, should be going off, sounding the alert that we are about to cross over into a place where we have no protection.

I've done this many times when I was flying. I would get into a "stall" situation, meaning I did not have enough airspeed to keep me aloft and was going to crash if I did not do something about it. Stall horns and red lights were my signals to do something about my situation or pay the consequences. I had ventured past the laws that said my airplane could fly no longer. It would nose dive into the ground. It was a choice. I had the controls. I had to do one of two things, crash or get out of my situation.

You too, have the controls (under God's control of course). Stay in your own backyard!

Here is another example taken from Scripture. Proverbs 10:4 (NKJV), "*He who has a slack hand becomes poor, But the hand of the diligent makes rich.*" There are two places you and I can live, a place in which "poor" follows us, or a place where "rich" follows us. God set up two parameters or borders, if you will. Poor and rich are choices; both have boundaries. If you stray from the one, you enter the other. One is good and the other is not. Certain disciplines, or the lack of them, will land you into one or the other of these two places. Again, it is all about choice.

Here is one more example. "*Hatred stirs up strife, But love covers all sins.*" (Proverbs 10:12 NKJV) When you hate, you have now crossed over into a territory that was not assigned you. When you love, you get to stay in your own backyard where God can keep an eye out for you.

We could go on and on as to what Scripture says about borders. I think you have the idea now, so let's move on.

Suffice it to say that when we venture out from under the wings of the Almighty and into unknown territories, we are in a "no mans land" and we will get into trouble. Many people who had given their lives to Christ in years past, decided all of a sudden, it wasn't worth it and went back to the world's way of doing things. They "crossed over" into a place they were not supposed to be. Some never returned. Don't let that be you! Stay in your own yard!

Job 38:10-11 (NKJV) says this, "*When I fixed my limit for it, And set bars and doors; When I said, 'This far you may come, but no farther, And here your proud waves must stop!'*"

If God set limits on the seas that He created, how much more so will He set limits for us? What would have happened if He had set no limits on the seas? The world would have run amuck. So will we if we are allowed to run without limits. It's strange to me that we think of God as one who limits our peace and fun. Not so. In Him we have fullness of joy. Pleasure abounds in Him. Peace is ours in Him. There are no limits when we are in Him. We impose our own limits. It starts in the mind.

"I can't do that. I can't go there." I can't, I can't, I can't. These are all self-imposed limits. Take the limits off God and let Him do in you what needs to be done. You would be surprised at how much freedom you will have. He will let you and I run as far as the "leash" of His Word will allow us. Once beyond that, we are pretty much on our own.

The prodigal son is just such an example. You can read the story in Luke 15:11-32. He wanted his stuff so Dad gave in to him. He left home only to waste all he had on "prodigal" living. Later he returns home which he should never have left in the first place. He began to be in want after all his money was gone. He winds up in the hog pen eating the hog's food that wasn't on his daily requirement of healthy foods.

We do that. We want to go beyond God's limits. We want to explore. Borders are set up to keep something in and keep something out. It could be people or animals. Borders do not shut out freedom. Real freedom is ours when we stay within the borders set up for us by God. These borders can be likened unto a corral. Wild horses are corralled. Before that, they had to fend for themselves. After being corralled they are broken (trained) and used for various purposes. They do not have to fend for themselves any longer. It is all handed to them. They never lost their freedom. Before being corralled, they were of little use. After being corralled AND trained, they were of tremendous value, especially in the old days. They pulled things, they hauled things and they ran races. They became one of man's best friends. But only after they had been trained did they become of value. Some, today, are worth millions. And some are just pets for little children.

We were like that, wild in the world. But God corralled us by giving us Jesus who saves us from the world. We are corralled and trained. We have not lost our freedom but gained everything that we did not possess in the world, freedom being one of them.

We do not like restrictions or to be restricted. "I am my own boss." I hear people saying that all the time. "It's my body. I can do what I want with it." Okay, be like the prodigal son. Have your way! You can live off the dregs of this world or the "riches" of God.

Corrals keep us in check. God's boundaries are found in His Word, and we can take the Word with us. We are corralled but free. The limits or restrictions travel with us.

Adam and Eve were given certain restrictions. "This you may eat but that over there, you may not eat." (My paraphrase) One involved freedom. They could have enjoyed the "good life". You know the rest of the story. They got kicked out of the "good life". Jesus comes along and hands it all back to us (abundant life) but with certain restrictions. All we have to do is follow the rules.

There are more "don'ts" in the Bible than there are "dos". I wonder why? I would say, probably for our own good. We are free to travel in the world but not free to travel the way of the world. The word bondage is found 39 times in the Bible. The words freedom and free are found 61 times. Maybe God wants us to be free more than to be in bondage. In the meantime, stay in your own backyard. God's watching you!

Chapter Thirteen

Traveling in Wrong Circles

The righteous should choose his friends carefully, for the way of the wicked leads them astray. (Proverbs 12:26 NKJV)

He who walks with wise men will be wise. But the companion of fools will be destroyed. (Proverbs 13:20 NKJV)

Wherefore come out from among them, and be ye separate, saith the Lord. (2 Corinthians 6:17a KJV)

As a young teen, my mother knew the pitfalls that lay ahead of me. Here is one of her "wisdom teachings". It was a lesson I was going to have to embrace and lay hold of much later in life. "William, if the gang you hang out with gets into trouble, and even though you were not actively part of the trouble, you, too, will be as much to blame as those who instigated the trouble." In other words, she was saying, "You'll pay the same price as those you hang out with." What great advice! And because I did not heed that advice early in my life, I eventually became a part of those whom she had told me to stay away from. And yes, I did in fact pay the same price as those whose lifestyle seemed more important than the words of a woman with much wisdom.

Have you noticed that the vast majority of people today are going around in circles? Even as I write this book, I've asked several people this question, "Have you ever gone around in circles?" Their reply was, "Sure have and still am. I can't seem to find my way off this merry-go-round. It's just one crazy ride after another." I followed with a second question. "Have you ever hung around with wrong people and wound up in trouble?" I wasn't surprised by their answer. "Yes, I have and it sure got me into a lot of trouble. I'm still fighting my way out of some of those predicaments."

You've no doubt heard this old saying, "Round and round she goes and where she stops nobody knows." Is that your story? If it is, perhaps this book will be of some help in getting you off those crazy merry-go-rounds and hanging out with wrong people. I sincerely hope it is a help to you and you get off the "ride without end" and start climbing to your God given destiny. In this particular chapter I will tell you how I got off track and on the merry-go-round and how I hung out with the crowd that my mother told me about early in my life. Though you may think my story not relative to your life, remember that this book, in time, will be read by millions, and there will be those whose lives will be changed because of it. That is my prayer for you today!

Have you ever been completely worn out just going around in circles and going nowhere fast? We all have at some point in our lives. I know I have. But it is quite another thing to go around in *wrong* circles and wear your self out; that spells double trouble. Not only are you going around in circles, you are going around in circles with the wrong crowd. Have you noticed how we change from one circle to another looking for that allusive hope, that certain something, that will free us from the captivity of the "circle"? "Well, this ain't getting me anywhere. I guess I'll try that other bunch. Somebody told me they were the "in" group. I might just as well try them. Nothing else is working for me."

What do I mean by, "Wrong circles"? The answer is simple. It's those circles of influence that lead to wrong places. It's those circles of influence that grab you and suck you into their way of living until they choke the very life out of you. Have you noticed that we tend to migrate towards those circles that look like they might be the most beneficial to us, right or wrong? We seldom check them out. "If I can just join the right club, I'll be somebody. I'll get noticed." Whatever sways you in wrong directions; those are the circles to stay out of. There are, of course, right and wrong circles. There are those circles that produce benefits for you and others. Then there are those circles that produce nothing but consequences. Those consequences stem from having made bad choices. However, bad choices are not failure. Here is what failure is; a few daily errors in judgment left unattended, resulting in chaos. Here is what failure is not; it is not a person, it is an event.

Watch out for what influences you the most. It may look good on the outside, but destruction lies on the inside, carefully camouflaged as good. The devil is a liar; nothing he can concoct is good, he just makes it sound good and look good. If it sounds too good to be true, then it probably is. Don't let wrong influences rub off on you. Be careful who you associate with. It's like brushing up against a flower that has pollen on it. The slightest brushing against the flower and the pollen is all over you. You carry it with you wherever you go. It's the same with people. You brush up against enough of those whose purpose is to do you in, and soon you will become like them. It all happens so subtly. Beware!

We are known by the company we keep. Have you noticed how we stay in certain groups? The young married people are in one group and the older in another. The singles mingle together. Certain professions hang out together. Particular career groups hang out together. We are identified by those groups we hang out with. We see it in churches. There is a class for every group and age. "What class do you go to?" "I go to the young married class." "And what class do you go to, sir?" "Well, I go to the senior men's group down the hall. There are just a few of us but we are so happy there in our little class." Baptists hang out with Baptists and the Methodist hang out with the Methodist and never the twain shall mix.

All circles, even though they have no end, go somewhere. It's their influence.

You are known by association. If the bunch you hang out with is known for their trouble making, you, too, will take on that association. You will take on their name. Don't let people name you. Associate with the kinds of people that will bear a good name.

Since we have been talking in this book about "going around in circles", and the futility of it all, I think it appropriate to talk some about the wrong circles we travel in, for they too, are futility. If you are traveling in circles that are of no benefit to you or others, and you refuse to get off those kinds of merry-go-rounds, you will wind up in the ditches of life; total despair, confusion and futility being your closest companions.

Wrong crowds can also be found in the spirit realm; yes, even in the Church. You must choose the group God wants you in. That's the group where God can pull the best out of you. All other groups only cause you to go around in circles. Over the years I found groups that were poverty minded. Then I found other groups who were just the opposite. I found groups that believed God does not heal anymore; that sickness and disease should be part of our lives and that God put it on us to teach us a lesson. Then I found the group that believes He does heal every kind of sickness and disease and that He wants to bless us with blessings unfathomable. I found groups that believed God is a cruel God, while others believe He is a loving Father. Then there are the misers and the givers. There are those who would rather lose their salvation than give up their denominational name tags. Then there are the stiff-necked ones who will not budge from their man-made rules and regulations. There are the groups that worship God without hindrance; caring less about what man might think. They are the ones who refuse to belong to any group. They are FREE! Be careful in the selection of the group you join. There are only two directions they can take you; up or down!

Once you've found your God-assigned group, that is, the place God has assigned you; you need to be aware of those who will try to infiltrate your group to once again, get you off track. They are called wolves but look like sheep. Sheep in the Bible are referring to God's children. Guess which group the wolves come from? Acts 20:29 (KJV) reads, "*For I know this, that after my departing shall grievous wolves enter in among you, not sparing the flock.*" Their assignment is simple. It is to separate the group; to get them milling around in circles not knowing in which direction to go. It is to divide and conquer and to cause disorder. Sheep do quite well as long as someone is leading them and keeping them in check. Once a sheep is separated from its group and the shepherd who is overseeing and protecting that group, it is easy prey for a wolf (the devil). Beware of wolves in sheep's clothing!

SUCCESS KEY -   It is essential that we hang out with the right people if we want God to bless us.

The date was January 16th, 1948. The place was my hometown of Bath, in the beautiful state of Maine. The event was my enlistment in the USAAF (United States Army Air Force for those too young to know what USAAF stands for). I had just signed on the dotted line at the U.S. Army Recruiting Office located in the City Hall on Front Street in Bath. The branch of service that you would be assigned, that is, the U.S. Army or U.S. Army Air Force, was determined by the results of an AGCT test. A score of 90 or below meant you were the property of the U.S. Army. Over 90 meant you belonged to the Air Force. FYI - The USAAF became the U.S. Air Force a few years later. My AGCT test score was 102 and so the U.S. Air Force was to become my home away from home for the next five years. A few days later, after the initial paperwork had been completed, I boarded a Greyhound bus bound for Boston, Massachusetts, where I was to take my physical. From there I traveled by train to Lackland Air Force Base in San Antonio, Texas. It was there I was to spend the next several months to be trained for military duty. After graduating from "boot camp", I went home for a short furlough and then received my orders to go to Camp Kilmer in New Brunswick, New Jersey. Kilmer was a POE (Point of Embarkation) camp where GI's left for duty all over the world. A few weeks later, after having arrived in Camp Kilmer, we were convoyed by truck to the Brooklyn Docks in New York and sailed from there to Bremerhaven, Germany, on the troop ship, Lt. J.B. Ray. That was a 21-day journey I shall never forget. We were so slow the Queen Mary passed us three times.

I spent the next year or so traveling to several bases in Germany and finally ended up on what had been a German Artillery Base that was located in Kaufbueren, Germany. After my tour of duty in the ETO (European Theater of Operations) it was back to stateside where I was stationed on several Air Force bases, one of which was Andrews Air Force Base. I ended up at U.S. Naval Quarters "K" in Arlington, Virginia, adjacent to Washington, D.C. Being Air Force property, how I arrived at a Navy Base is still a mystery to me. I was later discharged from the Air Force in D.C. and headed out into the non-military world. What a surprise that was! Being stationed at Naval Quarters "K" was a great experience. The Arlington National Cemetery was only a short distance away. I've been there several times. The Pentagon Building, where I worked for about a year on the 5th floor, "C" corridor (if my memory serves me right), was also just a short distance away.

After the military, I hung around the local area and finally went to work for Dr. Pepper Bottling Company, driving trucks and delivering their goods to stores, circuses, carnivals and what have you. But the destructive habits I had picked up during those young years were to lead me on paths that could have, and should have, ended my life, not once but several times. It is only by the grace of God, that I am here to tell you my story. Even five major accidents, any one of which should have killed me, did not abort the plan God had for my life.

I led a very quiet life as a youngster being raised by my adopted parents in Bath, Maine. Trouble started (I did not recognize it as trouble at the time) when I was allowed to go "up town" and hang out with some friends, most of which were from Morse High School which I had attended before the military nabbed me. But there were a few of the guys from the group I hung out with who were older than me. They had already graduated from high school and a couple of them were in the Armed Forces. These were also the guys who would buy beer for those of us too young to buy it. We would sneak under the Carlton Bridge in Bath, our secret place, where we would consume our "booty" and then "strut our stuff" for the girls. One of those older guys I remember. His name was Lewis. He was home on furlough from the U.S. Navy. When we had to "go" we would use the facilities found in the basement of the City Hall. On one of those much-needed visits, Lewis pulled a pint of whiskey out from under his jacket and offered me a drink.

Now you have to remember one thing; having been given up and given away at birth, having been born out of wedlock along with two other children, and not knowing who my biological father was, gave way to a tremendous lack in my life. It was called the "lack of love". I don't remember there being any love shown in those early years.

If there was, it was well hidden. From that stemmed the need to be loved and accepted so I gave in to whatever and who ever offered me love and acceptance.

So I took a drink from the bottle of whiskey that Lewis had offered me. It was my time to show off and be a real man at age sixteen. Between that time and the time I came back from Germany, I had already been married and divorced. I began hanging out with the wrong crowd. I sought that elusive "love" from wrong sources. Since "I love you" was a phrase not heard around my house, it was easily accepted from other sources. This early start of going down wrong roads would eventually cause me to search out those who were like what I was to become. I sought people who would fill the emptiness stemming from my bad start not realizing that only God could do that.

That drink of whiskey was not my first drink of alcohol. My dad, much to my mother's disagreement, would sometimes give me a glass of beer, generally at mealtime. "That won't hurt him. It's good for him. What harm can there be in giving him a glass of beer?" Little did he know the doors he was opening. Even parents today give their kids "drinks" at home. "They are going to drink any way, so why not give it to them at home," is their rational. Okay then; why not let them do drugs, have sex, steal, use profanity and whatever else comes to mind at home? "What harm could that possibly do? They're going to learn all about these things at school and other places, so why not let them have some at home? Let's "educate" them. We'll start at home. It will be much safer. Let's open their eyes to the dangers of it all." Parents, you have no idea what you are doing.

Because of the way I started out, and what I was NOT taught as a kid, permeated my next years after the military that was to take a strong grip on me and cause much trouble. I had had no father-and-son talks. After all, what were my adopted parents going to teach me? You cannot teach what you have not experienced and do not possess. My biological dad was unknown and my biological mother turned out to be my Aunt Florence. "C'mon now, how serious can a little thing like that be?" But it was to affect and infect me until April of 1976 when Jesus became Lord of my life. No, trouble did not depart all of a sudden; I am still a work in progress even at age 75, writing books that hopefully will help others from straying off the "narrow road" as I did and becoming all God desires us to become.

How did I get so far off track? By hanging out with those people who were going the same way I was; "Down the tubes". If you want to go up the ladder of success, you cannot hang out with those who are going down the tubes. Suffice it to pass each other on the way but YOU must keep on climbing while they head for destruction. You're reaching up for better things and the things of God. Their road is a "dead end".

On the train ride from Boston to Lackland Air Force Base in San Antonio, which would be my home for a few months for "boot camp", there was a short layover. During that time, some of the other kids who were older than I, and from the "big city", got off the train to buy booze. You know the rest of the story. If asked why I got involved with them, I would have told you, "I'm just trying to be one of the guys." "Hey, you over there, farmer boy, from Bath, Maine, come and live it up. Join us. Don't be a sissy all your life. Have a drink." "Okay, okay. You talked me into it." After all, no one told me how badly it could mess up my life, not my parents, not our pastor and none of my school teachers. It must have been okay. I mean, after all, they gave that stuff to me right in my own house. They drank, and besides that, they went to church. So how bad could that be? My dad was the Superintendent of the Sunday School Department and my mother was also in a leadership position. "C'mon, give me a break! They meant no harm." All my friends told me it was okay and I trusted them. They gave me the attention I needed. Since I found none at home, why not trust in those others; not knowing the pathway they were on was leading to a dead end.

I've told all this to show how easily you can get off track, off the narrow road. *"Because strait is the gate, and narrow is the way, which leadeth unto life, and few there be that find it."* (Matthew 7:14 KJV) My mother said this to me many times. "William, you better get on the straight and narrow." Little did I know what she meant by that statement. Later, when I had given my heart to the Lord she said, "Thank God, that boy has finally done something right", meaning, he has finally gotten on the "straight and narrow". What I did not know was how hard it was going to be to stay on that road. Nobody told me. They knew but they didn't feel it necessary to tell a boy from Bath, Maine, who had gotten a raw deal.

I do not blame anyone but myself for the choices I had made, not my parents, not my "born out of wedlock situation", not my teachers, not the military, not my friends, not the devil and certainly not God. I made the choices based on the information I had received and what I saw others doing. I started off by traveling in wrong circles and with the wrong people, all of which, the good and the bad, has led me to where I am now; writing books, and providing information about how to get out the ditches of life and move to higher grounds. The floodwaters of defeat cannot harm you if you are on higher grounds. Thank God, He made it all work together for good. (Romans 8:28)

It's like the Israelites traveling in the wilderness for 40 years when it should have taken them something less than two weeks. Ironically, I received the Lord at age 45, so it took me another five years of wandering around. Some people learn fast; others, well, let's just let that dog lie. But seriously, it is all in God's timing. He raises up one this way and another that way. God does not work in time. He is timeless. We are limited by time.

Now you remember what Scripture says in John 10:10. (KJV) *"The thief cometh not, but for to steal, and to kill, and to destroy: I am come that they might have life, and that they might have it more abundantly."*

Wouldn't you think a person would get tired of having things stolen from them, of being on a "hit" list and destruction following then everywhere they go?

My story is only one of millions. It doesn't have to be booze that gets you off track. In my case, it got hold of me before I ever found the track. That is how the devil steals from you. He catches young people unaware. They have only their parents to teach them and get them headed in the right direction. Parents, do your children right, teach them the Word of God early on. When they are headed for the wrong crowd, stop them! *"Train up a child in the way he should go; and when he is old he will not depart from it.* (Proverbs 22:6 KJV) My parents were in church but they did not know the Word of God. What were they going to teach me? All they had to go on was a few tidbits they had heard perhaps in a sermon. They were ignorant of the Word of God. Ignorance is not bliss. Ignorance means you have not been informed. They had not been informed and were too busy, in those days, making ends meet. Today is a different story. We have all we need to teach our kids and keep them away from those "wrong crowds". Too many parents today are teaching their opinion, not the Word of God. They're teaching the world's way to do things and we are in a mess. We've got wrong crowds everywhere. There is no shortage of wrong crowds. Make sure your children are not headed that way. For that matter, make sure you are not; you are their example. Who else have they got? If they don't have you, they have the world to help them get off track. Get your kids off the merry-go-rounds and stop them from hanging out with wrong crowds. When they are older, you will be glad you did and they will praise you for it.

SUCCESS KEY: Choose your friends carefully. Walk with the wise and be separated from the world's way of doing things.

Chapter Fourteen

Get Rid of the Clutter

"I would move on but for the clutter in my life. It keeps holding me back from what God has promised." Dr. B

A few years ago I moved from an apartment I had lived in for nineteen years to another part of Houston. I had not realized how much I had accumulated in personal possessions. I should have recognized it early on since I had to walk like a crab, sideways, to make it around my "stuff". The enormity of my gatherings and what to do with it all overwhelmed me. Some I could discard, but what? Once the process of packing started, I quickly realized that I would have to give or throw away some things and not carry that clutter with me. However, it seemed the more I threw away, the more it revealed things that needed to be thrown away. More and more "stuff" just came to the surface. I finally made it to my other location minus what would have amounted to several large boxes of clutter. I had not realized that clutter in your life can add unnecessary burdens, many of which we will talk about here in this chapter.

When you get rid of the clutter in your life, it will reveal God's blessings. It is His job to point you to the clutter. It is your job to do something with it. You can keep it or get rid of it. It's your choice.

- Clutter in your life reveals the character in you. It reveals who and where you are. It reveals what you are. It tells a story to everyone who is watching you.

- Clutter overwhelms you because you don't know what to do with it when it has overtaken you.

- Clutter grows. If you pay no attention to it at first, it will only continue to grow. It will overtake you, outgrow you, overwhelm you, confuse you and soon it will bury you.

- Clutter contaminates. Once it is allowed to grow, it reaches out and contaminates everything you do.

- Clutter coagulates the flow of God's blessing. It stops the free flow of blessings.

- Clutter is the weed that grows alongside the rose bush, and if allowed to, it will soon take over the life intended for the rose and kill it.

- Clutter chokes off the room God intended for blessings to come. When clutter overtakes a place, it takes up the space God had intended for you to bloom and blossom in.

- Clutter removed reveals what is underneath.

- Clutter dims the vision.

- Clutter obscures what lies beyond it.

- Clutter is an obstacle, which if allowed to grow, soon outgrows the will to remove it.

- Clutter is not what you save for a rainy day hoping to eventually find some use for it.

- Clutter is not cool. It is a waste of space.

- Clutter will soon slow you down, and then stop you altogether. That's when the devil gets a shot at you. It's not hard for him to hit a target that has quit moving.

How many valuable pieces of furniture have been discovered once the clutter was removed? Have you ever visited the flea markets and garage sales looking for a bargain? I have many times. You find a piece of furniture but you cannot identify it because it is covered with clutter. You remove the clutter. What was under the it is now revealed, but you have one more step to go. You must remove the several coats of paint, which were used to cover up the blemishes from the years of wear. Now it is fully revealed. What was under it all is a fine piece of furniture, valuable and to be treasured.

This is what happened in my life; thirty years ago you would not have seen the writer and teacher in me because there was too much clutter. There were many coverings that had to be removed to reveal the gifts and talents in me. I did not know there was a writer and teacher in me but God did and so He started the restoration process. Here we are thirty years later and those gifts are constantly being uncovered, one layer at a time. By the way, I still have a way to go. I've not arrived yet but am on the way.

Over the years I have accumulated a lot of road film, but God has the "road film remover". It is called the Word of God. As each layer of accumulation is removed, God's intention for our lives is revealed. Not too much at once, else pride gets in the way, but just enough to let you know He is on the job. Sometimes a little "hide" comes off with the cleaning process. But, hurt as it may, God knows just how much "peeling away" we can stand.

It's like the wound we want to pick at as it scabs over to see what's underneath. We try to hasten the process of healing (God's process) but doing more harm than good. All we find is that it is not yet healed. If we dig around too much we will find there is still pain underneath it all waiting for a healing touch from The Master's Hand.

Most of the time those layers and accumulations are sin and He must get to the root of it all. Too many people treat symptoms while God treats the cause which is the root of it all. All He wants to do is uncover what lies beneath. It is called His gift to us. It is what He created us for. He simply wants to uncover what He gave us in the beginning. Since we are made in His Image, He simply wants to reveal that in us. He wants to uncover that image and reveal to the world Himself in us.

We have yet to know all that God has in store for us. We are limited in our own power; He is limitless. Our prayer should be, "God, do in me what I cannot do for my self. Search me and create in me a clean heart, one that is pleasing to you. Remove all the clutter so that You might be revealed to others through me. Uncover what lies beneath, the good and the bad. Uncover me, Lord; expose the bad to reveal the gifts within. Uncover me that Your light might shine through me so that others might know You."

What have you allowed to clutter your life? What have you allowed that has been holding you back to what God has in store for you? What trinkets have you kept and treasured so much that they have overtaken you and hid from view what God has in store for you?

Clutter, of course, comes from our past and it is one of the most dangerous kinds of clutter. Clutter buries things, one of which is truth. And truth revealed makes people free (John 8:32). Truth is all around us but covered by clutter. To get to the truth of a matter, we must uncover it. The Bible says we are to *know* the truth, not just let it lie around hoping someday it will find us. This is such an important issue. I've mentioned it several times here in this book and it needs to be addressed again.

Many times we let the clutter pile up in our lives, in order to not have to deal with the truth of a matter. If it is hidden from view, I can't see it and I do not have to deal with it. Out of sight, out of mind, is our thinking; but isn't it ironic that many of the things we try our best to hide, somehow come to the surface. Why? So that the issue might be dealt with. There is something there that God wants revealed in us that He may shine through us. It is like that piece of furniture we found tucked away in the back of the antique store. It didn't look like much before we purchased it and gave it a good cleaning, but look at it now.

There is another area we must touch on. There is a television show that comes on Monday night here in Houston. Items that have been brought in are appraised by experts for their potential value. Some people made the trip for nothing. They went home with their prized "whatchamacallit", it having no value. But there are some pieces that bring millions. Here is an example. A fine piece of furniture has been discovered. It is covered with years of dirt, grime and what have you. In its journey through time, it has gathered some "road film". The purchaser of this fine piece of furniture does not realize its value and removes the dirt and grime hoping to reveal the original finish. What they do not realize is this. They have removed the most valuable part and it has drastically reduced the value. Why? The character is gone. What once was very valuable is now lost for ever and can never be replaced. It is called persona, meaning character, the façade, and the beauty of it all. Its history has been erased forever. So, in the case of this piece of antique furniture, you do not remove the persona and character. By doing this, the furniture keeps its value for years to come. In fact, many times it will increase in value with age. Many times, a piece like this will become priceless; a national treasure. No amount of value can be placed on it. Its one of a kind and there is none like it.

Let this sink into your being. You are one of a kind! There is none like you. I can hear some of you saying, "You got that right, Bill. I sure am one of a kind. I've messed up so badly. There is no hope for a person like me." Let me respond to that. "Yes, there is! There is always hope and it is found only in Jesus." There are no "hopeless" cases for Him. He can and does restore what has been thrown away and cast aside by society.

Here is how He does it. He removes the outer to reveal the inner you. It is just the opposite of the piece of antique furniture we just talked about. For that priceless piece of furniture, we leave the dirt, grime and road film that has built up over the years in tact. God does the opposite. He removes it because He wants to reveal what is underneath it all. He strips away more of the outer which reveals the inner beauty. You and I become more valuable; priceless. Before meeting Christ as Lord and Savior there wasn't much hope, but as God peels away the outer layers of sin, He reveals Himself on the inside. He simply wants to clean up the house He has been invited to come live in.

"Therefore if any man be in Christ, he is a new creature: old things are passed away; behold, all things are become new." (2 Corinthians 5:17 KJV)

Chapter Fifteen

Make Up Your Mind

"A double minded man is unstable in all his ways."
(James 1:8 KJV)

"…but be transformed by the renewing of your mind…" (Romans
12:2a NKJV)

People, who are going around in circles trying to figure life out,
do so because they are double minded and unstable; there is more
doubt than faith and the two are not compatible. You confuse your
mind when you cannot make up your mind who and Whose you
are. Every time you make a turn on the proverbial merry-go-round
saying, "I don't know who I am, I don't know who I am, I don't know
who I am," you are ordering failure. God says you are blessed and
highly favored and you say, "No way. That doesn't apply to me."
If not you, then who is He blessing? "Well, the ones who were
born on the right side of the track; you know, the side opposite of
me." Consider this; since God is no respecter of people (and He
isn't because He loves all people), who would He leave out of His
blessing? Only those who think they cannot be blessed by Him. If
your mind is made up that God will not bless you, then that is what
you will receive. When you pick up one end of the stick, you also
get the end opposite. I can hear some of you saying, "See, I told you
He wouldn't bless me. I said He wouldn't and He didn't, so there.
I was right." Here is a good Scripture for you found in Proverbs
18:20-21 (KJV), *"A man's belly shall be satisfied with the fruit of his
mouth; and with the increase of his lips shall he be filled. Death and life
are in the power of the tongue: And they that love it shall eat the fruit
thereof."*

If you tell your mind today that you are going to be successful and then tomorrow you tell it you are a failure, you have cancelled the first thought of being successful by the second thought; I am a failure. You simply have ordered chaos. Your mind screams at you, "Make up your mind. I don't know what you want. You've tied my hands. I cannot bring you both. Tell me what you want and stick to your guns." People wear themselves out trying to figure it out. They vacillate between two thoughts, neither of which is compatible with the other. One leads you up the mountain, while the other keeps you in the ditch. Should I take a left or should I take a right?

Have you ever watched someone make a turn at the last minute and it almost caused an accident? They could not make up their mind which way to turn until the last minute and then while making the turn say, "I should have turned the other way."

Joshua reminded the Israelites about what Moses had commanded them (See Joshua 1:7) when he said (paraphrased) "Don't turn to the right hand or the left hand. You know what to do, now do it. Don't turn from what I have commanded you. Stay on the path that will make your way prosperous and then you will have good success. If you do, you will not fail." The word "success" in this Scripture means to handle effectively the affairs of life or act wisely in the affairs of life. You can do neither going around in a circle bemoaning life as not fair. You cannot act wisely by being double minded – unable to make up your mind. It's like the person who is handed a plate full of assorted goodies. "Now let's see. Which shall I take?" So they take one of each unable to make up their minds.

We fail when we take the wrong path, but who is to know which the right path is? Well, God does! He has been gracious enough to leave the directions for success (see definition of success above) written down in black and white; it's called the Bible. It gives positive direction for our lives. How well we follow those guidelines determines our success and/or failure rate. It not only tells us how to stay out of trouble, it also gives direction as to what to do when we get in trouble, and we will; believe me when I say that. Trouble lurks on both sides of the road to success.

One of the reasons people fail in life is because they will not stay on the right path once it's known. Of course, it may take a while to figure out what that path is. When you have your assignment from God, don't turn from it unless you want failure to beat you back into the ditches of life.

Who are you? Who am I? You are either who God says you are, or you are not. To say you are not who God says you are, is to make Him a liar and His Word not true. If He says you're a winner than you are; nowhere in the Bible does He say you are a loser. There are many places where the Bible says you lose if you do such and such a thing after having been warned against it, but it doesn't call you a loser. It many times, however, calls you a fool. He says you and I are more than conquerors (over comers) in Christ Jesus. To be a conqueror is one thing; it is still another to be more than a conqueror. "More than" means to go one step further and beyond the norm of things.

> **SUCCESS KEY –** **What and who you once were, you are no longer. If you are growing (mentally, physically, and spiritually), then you cannot be today who you were yesterday; therefore, continue to grow!**

> **SUCCESS KEY -** **Decisions can deepen my problems or release my progress. You can make the decision to agree with God which will release progress, or to disagree with God and that will only deepen your problems.**

Here is what Scripture says about us, "*Therefore if any man be in Christ, he is a new creature: old things are passed away; behold, all things are become new.*" (II Corinthians 5:17 KJV)

We generally base how we see ourselves on performance, but performance has nothing to do with it. If you say you are less than what God says you are one day and something else the next day, you are fooling yourself. The devil has a game, a strategy if you will. He wants you to see everything you do based on past performance; but if the Scripture above is true, then it isn't about performance.

It is about what God has done. When we come to Christ and ask Him into our hearts, the inner man changes. (Romans 10:9-13) Our spirit (inner man) is reborn or, born again from above. When the spirit of a man has been reborn, he is a new creature. (John 3:3) Not so with the flesh, the outer man. It stays the same as it has always been. Believe me when I say the flesh wants to rule. The outer man is the culprit. It wars against the inner man. Whatever is the more dominant of the two will give direction. If the flesh (outer man) is more dominant, it gives way to destruction. If the spirit (inner man) is the more dominant, it gives way to life.

But aren't we all performance oriented to a certain extent? Little children perform for praises from others. My daughter, Karen, would ask me after a particular event, "Daddy, did I do well? Are you proud of me?"

The raises we receive at work (I call it the place of opportunity) are given on performance. We are performance rated. A product is sold based on its performance. A race car driver, after winning the race says, "The cars engine performed well." However, performance is not what God is interested in. You can't perform your way into a great deal with Him. He isn't interested. It's called works. You cannot work your way into good standing with Him. It all must come through the Cross of Calvary. (Eph. 2:8-9) It all begins at the Cross because the ground is level at the Cross for who so ever will come.

Companies give performance raises periodically. The raise is based on what you have done (past tense). They are hoping that, based on past performance, you will perform accordingly in the future. As a matter of fact, they are counting on it. They have just invested in your future based on your past performance. They want a good return on their investment.

God does not invest in our future based on our past performance. If He did, we would all be in some serious trouble. God is not looking at our past performances. He looks to our future. He looks at the shed blood of Jesus.

If we did well at day's end, we call that a successful day and give ourselves an extra "atta boy". Same day performed poorly and we call life a bummer and see ourselves as failures. That's because we sell ourselves a bill of goods based on how well or poorly we performed in any given day. In years past, when a day went down the tubes, I would have a few "pick me up's" – booze, on the way home and by the time I arrived at home things looked much better. Of course, all I had accomplished was the deepening of an already existing problem; one of poor self image. When you get the image right (Genesis 1:26-28), your days will be successful. When you get the image right, God blesses you (Genesis 1:28). Notice that God blessed *after* the image was right. He considered you and me (got the image right) and then created us for His purpose, which was to subdue, have dominion and multiply. Far too many complain today about the image. "God sure messed up when He created me (looking at self in a mirror). I don't like what I see. I'll just go and rearrange what God has created." After billions have been spent, we find it to be all in vain because the inner image is the same. Only the outer image has been altered, hoping it would change the inner man but it never does. Only God can do that through a relationship with Jesus Christ. If you don't like the way you were born, get born again (John 3). That way you will see yourself in a much better light, in the light of the Cross. Now you can let your light shine (Matthew 5:16).

For those whose day wasn't quite what you expected; life is not a bummer. Just because you didn't get that raise, that promotion, or what you thought you had deserved, doesn't make life any less. Life (in Christ) is to be enjoyed and it can be if you will get a clearer image of yourself.

You must make up your mind and to do that you must stop saying, "I am so confused about life. I'm not sure about anything anymore. I don't know where I am going. Nothing is working. Life's a bummer. I quit!" No, you must be smarter than that. Make up your mind. Do something so out of the ordinary for God that even if you failed, it would be worth it. I would rather do something great for God and fail then do nothing and succeed. "Bill, you sure don't know anything about my past, do you." There you go again, listening to the wrong voice. Here is a success tip for you. When the devil brings up your past, remind him of his future. (Rev. 20:10)

Stop hanging around those merry-go-rounds and do something big for God. Don't be a daydreamer.

SUCCESS KEY – Dreams without action are illusion.

To make up your mind means you tell it not what it wants to hear, but what it needs to hear to accomplish those God-given goals. If you tell your mind you want donuts tomorrow morning, you'll probably get the donuts against your better judgment. However, if you tell it what it needs to hear based on your goals, you'll get that too. "I want to climb the Enchanted Rock in Fredericksburg, Texas; therefore, donuts are not on my list of healthy things to eat to keep up the strength I will need to make that climb." You keep that focus in mind, taking no short cuts to the donut shop that is just a block away.

In view of that, let me introduce you to a guy named RAS. RAS means "Reticular Activating System." It's a four-inch network of cells radiating from our brain cells. Now for those super religious folks, who complain about everything, saying that it isn't God, remember He is the One who created RAS. RAS is our obedient slave - our robot, if you please. Your RAS never tells you what to do. You are in charge, and it does only what you ask of it. It will take negative or positive input and the only thing RAS is concerned about is how important that input is to you. If you say you are a failure then you have sent RAS direct orders to block out all success thoughts you originally had. When you say, "I am a winner", you send orders to RAS to block out all negatives relating to success. RAS is only interested in what dominates your thinking and what is important to you. RAS will get you your goals. It's your challenge to find out what to do with them after you get them. Want a new car? Is it your dominating thought? Then RAS gets it for you, but you have to figure out how to pay for it. Don't send RAS messages of what you don't want to do. Tell RAS what you want to do and intend on doing and follow through with it. Instead of saying, "I don't want to overeat," say, "I am getting in shape, therefore I won't overeat." He understands what you tell him. Just be careful! Remember, you are in charge, and he is the one taking orders from you. Build a hierarchy of thoughts; the latter being the most dominant will override those thoughts previous. Build enough positive thoughts and they will override all negatives, such that, you won't remember them any more. They will disappear into the recesses of your mind.

> **SUCCESS KEY -   Life and death are in the power of the tongue (Proverbs 18:20-21). Use it wisely.**

One reason why we fail so often is because we are not fully persuaded that we are winners. "After all, how could a person like me with such a distorted past, be a winner?" One day we are persuaded, the next not so. Why? It's because we have received information to the contrary. You can tell yourself, "You know you can't win. It's never been done before." or, "Good, I won't have any competition; therefore, I can do this and win. It may take me awhile to figure this thing out, but I'm on my way. Look out, clear the way, I'm coming through."

Here are a few examples of being persuaded and fully persuaded. *He (Abraham) staggered not at the promise of God through unbelief; but was strong in faith, giving glory to God; And being fully persuaded that, what he had promised, he was able also to perform.* (Romans 4:20-21 KJV)

"Let every man be fully persuaded in his own mind." (Romans 14:5b KJV)

"Then Agrippa said to Paul, *'You almost persuade me to become a Christian.'"* (Acts 26:28 NKJV) The key word here is "almost" but not fully persuaded. That's where most people are in life. They are not fully persuaded that they are winners. "Maybe I'll win today, but there is always tomorrow. I'll probably lose. You never know about tomorrow." Well, if you don't know about tomorrow, read the Book. It tells you all about tomorrow.

"And when he would not be persuaded, we ceased, saying, The will of the Lord be done." (Acts 21:14 KJV) You can talk just so much. Actions always follow instructions; otherwise you invite failure. My mother would say, "William, go clean your room." Now, either I

acted on her instruction, or she acted on my hinder parts, end of story!

"For I am persuaded, that neither death, nor life, nor angels, nor principalities, nor powers, nor things present, nor things to come, Nor height, nor depth, nor any other creature, shall be able to separate us from the love of God, which is in Christ Jesus our Lord. (Romans 8:38-39 KJV)

Another word for persuaded is convinced. You are either fully convinced or you are not.

> **SUCCESS KEY – Never see yourself on a vertical scale, you on the bottom and all others above you. Always see yourself horizontally; no one is above, no one is beneath, but all things are under God! "Don't rank me fourth and out of the race. I might be in fourth but look out, I'm moving up to a front line position; a number one."**

> **SUCCESS KEY –   See where you are going by faith while facing your past with reality.**

Make up your mind that God is after the good in you. Here is a neat story as best as I can remember it. A man was out strolling one day and happened to pass by another who was chipping away with hammer and chisel on a large piece of granite. Thinking this rather strange, the passerby asked the man what he was doing. He said, "I'm just removing some of the outer layers of this granite." "Why," the spectator asked. "So I can reveal the finer work which is on the inside." Even though this is not actually the way the story was told me (I'm having a senior moment) it does, in fact, reveal what God is doing to each of us if we will let Him. Make up your mind, today, to let God do what needs to be done to reveal what He has already placed on the inside. He chips away at the outer layers to reveal what He has placed inside us from the very beginning.

Jeremiah 1:5 (NIV) declares, *"Before I formed you in the womb I knew you, before you were born I set you apart."*

Psalms 139:14 (KJV) states, *"I will praise thee; for I am fearfully and wonderfully made: marvelous are thy works; and that my soul knoweth right well."*

Jeremiah 29:11 (NIV) says, *"For I know the plans I have for you,"* declares the LORD, *"plans to prosper you and not to harm you, plans to give you hope and a future."*

> ➢ We are blessed and highly favored.
> ➢ We are the head and not the tail.
> ➢ We are above and not beneath.
> ➢ We are seated in heavenly places.
> ➢ We are made a littler lower than the angels.
> ➢ We shall not lack for any good thing.
> ➢ He prepares a table for us even in the midst of our enemies.
> ➢ He makes us to lie down in green pastures.
> ➢ He restores us.
> ➢ He redeems us.
> ➢ He saves us.
> ➢ He heals us.
> ➢ We do not have to live in fear.
> ➢ We have the mind of Christ.

You cannot ask for much more than that.

God had a plan for you and me long before we ever came into this world and they are good plans. He means us no harm and wants to prosper us. Prosper means to have everything needed to do what God has called you to do and then some. It's the "then some" I like. It is the icing on the cake. It's the "more than enough" and God takes great delight in the prosperity of His children. Shalom! Nothing missing, nothing broken, this is what God wants for His children. I would say that is a winning plan. It is a win-win situation where no one loses. God put into you and I the will to win. When we do, we hand the winnings all back to Him. It's called the "Law of Mutual Exchange". God wins by getting the very best out of us and we win because we get to give it all back to Him so He can repeat the process. It is not a one-time plan where it is implemented just once and then stops. No, it is a plan for your life. God will never stop blessing you if you will just stay on track with Him.

All we have to do is come into agreement with God as to what and who He says we are. To not agree means we are going in a direction opposite of God. Two cannot agree when going in opposite directions. By not being in agreement with Him we are simply saying to God, "You go Your way and I'll go mine because my plan is better."

One of my favorite pastimes as a youngster was to read the "funnies" in our local Sunday newspaper. The heading on this newspaper is interesting, bearing out what I just said in the preceding paragraph. "What fools these mortals be."

Renew your mind today. "*And be not conformed to this world: but be ye transformed by the renewing of your mind, that ye may prove what is that good, and acceptable, and perfect, will of God.*" (Romans 12:2 KJV)

Agree with God that what and who He says you are, you are indeed. You'll never be the same! Never, never, never!

Chapter Sixteen

Adjusting Your Sights

"A person, who makes daily course corrections and adjustments, will be far more successful than the person who is careless (care-less) about life." Dr. B

"The abundant life Jesus spoke of in John 10:10 will be experienced by those who are always adjusting their sights to the truth that life was meant to be good." Dr. B

People who are going around in circles have simply missed the target; they aimed too low. They did not focus on their future, but rather their pasts. Their sights were not aligned with their future. Failure beckoned and they succumbed to it, thinking all their failures meant but one thing; they were a failure, doomed to a life of "less than" rather than a life of "more than". Not true! They simply missed the target because they aimed too low.

It's like the inexperienced duck hunter I once knew. We'll call him John. John didn't know the muzzle of a gun from the stock, or sights from the trigger. He only knew that a gun went "Bang". We had gone duck hunting one day, and upon arrival at our site, quickly concealed ourselves in some make-shift blinds and waited the arrival of those feathered flying, hard to hit birds, called ducks. The temperature was below zero. It was colder than cold: wet, wintry and very uncomfortable. In other words, it was an average day for duck hunting. Suddenly, and just under the canopy of dark grey clouds to our left, ducks appeared from seemingly nowhere. That's what ducks do, ya know. John, wanting to quit and go somewhere warm; jumped up, pointed his shotgun skyward and pulled the trigger, not once, but several times hitting nothing. (The ducks probably said jokingly amongst themselves, "Don't worry, it's only John.") I yelled, "John, what in the world are you doing? Ya gotta take aim at something. You just can't point your gun in the air and expect to hit any ducks." John said, "I thought all you had to do was point your gun in the general vicinity of those ducks and you were bound to hit one. Guess I was wrong." Actually, John hit his target. He aimed at nothing and hit it!

Here is your success key for the week. Aim at nothing and you will be 100% successful every time because you will hit absolutely nothing. Zero plus zero equals zero. You cannot shotgun your way to success. You have to set your sights on the target, taking careful aim and then squeeze the trigger.

Success is like that to some – not that important but let's take a shot at it anyway. After all, one more time around the mountain won't hurt. One more turn of the merry-go-round just might be our lucky turn. Who knows? One more lottery ticket might just solve all our problems.

The person who is relentless and passionate about life, has purpose and pursues godly ambitions, will win every time. Sure, there might be a few setbacks, but setbacks to those people are only to survey what went wrong and reconnoiter for a stronger push toward their God-given potential and destiny. Setbacks to others, is to set back in the recliner and let life go by (bye-bye, that is). Opportunity waves as it goes by one more time, unused, wasted; and failure, once again, has its way.

If you are constantly hitting nothing, after having done all you knew to do, it might mean that your sights need a little adjusting. In some cases, a major adjustment might be your key to success. If all else fails, throw the gun away and get another and get a new prospective on the subject you are pursuing. Starting over from where you are, not where you failed might be your answer.

Here is a success hint. The most expensive gun in the world is nothing more than something to be hung on a wall for others to admire if its sights are not properly adjusted. It is useless as far as its intended purpose. Sadly, it will be your only trophy. You will not have any stories of how the "big one" got away; so it is with success. If you do nothing more than read the books, listen to the audio tapes, view the DVD's, and go to the seminars; you will only get to "hang it on the wall" along with the rest of the trophies hanging there, the things you should have done, but did not. Success demand action on your part.

A gun owner knows the value of keeping his firearms in perfect condition. If a gun has been stored for any length of time, the first thing the owner must do and should do when the hunting season approaches, is to take his or her gun to the gun shop and have it checked over for any misalignment of its sights or scope. Sometimes a gun can have its sights accidentally knocked out of whack just in the transportation of it from one place to another. A little bump here, a little bump there and you come home empty handed after a hunting trip. Why? All because you neglected to have your sights adjusted before embarking on your trip.

> **SUCCESS KEY – Make certain your success sights are properly aligned before your trip, not after. It will be too late in many cases; your "trophy" will have disappeared. You may never get another "shot" at it.**

> **SUCCESS KEY – Don't take too long aiming at your success target. Once your target is identified, pull the trigger else your prize will get away.**

I can remember only too well, the deer I missed by hesitating, trying to identify my target. The deer, sensing there was no eminent danger, simply ambled off into the woods knowing there wasn't anything to fear from the inexperienced hunter (me). Though my gun was pointed in the general direction of the deer for the "shot of a lifetime", there would be no trophy that day to hang on the wall. But many are the trophies on the walls of inexperience and failure for those who refuse to make the necessary adjustments in life for their "prize". The Apostle Paul said (paraphrased), "I push on for the prize. I may have missed a few, but I've got to keep on moving forward regardless."

SUCCESS KEY - If it ain't working, then something is wrong. Fix it!

Have you been missing your targets more than hitting them? Is the bull's eye too small? No, the bull's eye is not too small; your perception of it is. Are you too far away from your target? Maybe you need to move closer to your target rather than it moving closer to you. That may involve some risk, but move anyway. Are you not seeing things clearly? Do your glasses need adjusting? No, you do not need new glasses. If you are not seeing your success target clearly, maybe you are looking through the wrong set of eyes. Maybe your vision is impaired by the winds of adversity, or you are looking though the eyes of past failures and performances. Perhaps you are looking at your rear view mirror more than you are looking though your windshield. Looking through your rear view mirror only shows you what has happened; looking through your windshield is a panoramic view of where you are going. Both eyes must be used to look forward; not one looking back while the other looks forward. You cannot see it two directions at once.

Now there are two sides to every coin. Let's look at the other side of the rear view mirror/windshield theory. A glance in the rear view mirror (past) might reveal something sneaking up on you or perhaps we should say someone. Enter stage right, the devil. He will not come at you headlong. He is a very sneaky adversary. The Bible says we are to not be ignorant of the schemes of the devil. If you cannot detect him moving up behind you, you might be in some serious trouble when he attacks. A glance every now and then in the rear view mirror might be wise, but don't look there too long. Don't focus on the devil. I know some people who do. You cannot focus on the devil and God at the same time. Just be aware that the devil is out there (1st Peter 5:8) seeking whom he may devour. If he can catch you unawares, he has you. Seek God first and foremost. Give the devil none of your time.

Now here is something you may not be aware of. A peek into your rear view mirror might reveal something other than your past. Here's what the younger generation might say. "It ain't all bad." Here is what we should be looking for. *"Surely goodness and mercy shall follow me all the days of my life..."* (Ps. 23:6 KJV) Have you ever heard that? Sure you have! Isn't that a good thing to be looking for? Wouldn't you like goodness and mercy to be following you instead of the devil nipping at your heals? The NIV Bible says it this way, "Surely goodness and love will follow me all the days of my life." Regardless of those errors in judgment, there is something good to come out of it all. God works all things together for good and for His purpose. How about this one? Deuteronomy 28:2 (KJV) reads, *"And all these blessings shall come on thee, and overtake thee, if thou shalt hearken unto the voice of the LORD thy God."* If something is going to overtake you, then it must have been behind you. Watch out! You are about to be blessed! It is about to overtake you!

Let's go back to adjusting our sights. Even when the sights and scope of a gun are properly aligned, yes, even then, there will be a few misses. We've all heard about the "big one, the trophy" that got away. Here's why it got away. Here is how success eludes us. We never expected goodness and mercy to follow us; we never expected God's blessings to come up from behind and overtake us. We never expected God to work all things together for good (Romans 8:28). "I failed again. Can any good thing come from this?" The answer is, yes, it can and will if you will expect the goodness of God to overtake you even when you are wrong. God will pursue you relentlessly to give you the best of life. He will send His "Hounds of Heaven" to search you out and bless you if you will but trust Him. God isn't trying to prove us wrong. He is proving that He is right, and was all along. We just had our sights misaligned to hear correctly, His advice for the better than good life.

Missing the intended mark for our lives does not mean we are failures; it means we aimed too low and missed God's best for our lives, but His best is still available. God did not take it away from us. Delayed, yes, but not denied. All you have to do is aim higher, my friend, aim higher.

Here are some critical success keys that perhaps you have never considered:

- Keep doing what you're doing. Eventually, you'll get it right.

- Remember that failure is temporary, an interruption, and an inconvenience while on your way to success.
- Don't ever quit!
- Stay focused and on course.
- Don't make your mistakes an issue, and don't let the devil make an issue of them either.
- Make room for success by forgetting your errors in judgment after having learned from them.
- Pray for wisdom. It is the principle thing.
- Let God handle your past. You've already messed up enough.
- Look for something new in life. God just might have a surprise in store for you.

Let me ask you something. We're still talking about success and hitting your intended target. Remember that the title of this particular chapter is, "Adjusting Your Sights". Here is the question; can you aim too high? Well, the answer is both yes and no. Before we get into aiming too high, let's look at aiming too low and move up from there. You can aim too low and hit everything *except* your intended target. That is the problem with most people. They excel at aiming too low in life, hitting nothing. You will be known as the person who hits nothing or no-thing every time. The duck hunter we spoke of earlier aimed skyward and shot at the sky hoping he might hit something. The target was there, which was the ducks, but he did not aim at the ducks. It's like the person who shuts their eyes when they pull the trigger. You might as well shut your eyes because the reward is the same when aiming at nothing as it is when shutting your eyes, just blindly hoping. You're hoping something will accidentally run into your bullet rather than the bullet hitting the bull's eye.

But for the person who aims too high, can they hit their target? Let's put it this way; the chances are much better than if you aimed too low. Aiming too high might just "bag your limit". Let me explain.

The trajectory of a bullet, when leaving the muzzle of a gun, is in an upward arc. It goes up (slightly) and then downward, leveling off, traveling toward its target. If a target was a long way off, you would aim slightly higher than the bull's eye because of this trajectory. If you aimed too high you would probably hit the upper portion of the outer rings of your target. If you aimed too low you would probably hit the lower portion of the outer rings of your target. In either case, too high or too low, will bring a negative result, missing the target altogether. There is a point of no return. Too high you miss and too low you miss.

I asked this question earlier; can you aim too high? I answered it by saying both yes and no. Aim too low and you walk away without the prize. Aim too high and you could walk away with the prize because aiming too high, or aiming for something that is beyond your reach causes you to stretch beyond your own capacities and capabilities, but at least aim high. Who knows what you might hit? Too low and you hit nothing.

> **SUCCESS KEY - Great success is always higher than the person who is always aiming too low. For the person who aims high, success is much closer than the person who is always aiming too low. Success is never beneath but above you, causing you to reach higher for the abundant life.**

It's like buying a book and never reading it. Nothing ventured, nothing gained. You aimed too low. But for the person who buys the book and reads it, that is another story. What if you did not understand the book the first time you read it? Then you reach higher and read it again. It may take a third and fourth time, but if you reach high enough you will eventually understand its contents. Each time you read, you are reaching higher.

Here is a personal example. I wrote my first book, which was titled, "Journey to the Top". I could have stopped there, aiming too low, but I didn't. I wrote another, aiming higher for a best seller. The best seller did not come from the first book but it will come from what I write after that. At some point in time, if I reach high enough, I will write a best seller. And I'll even reach higher than that, writing a second and a third best seller until all the books inside me are published for the world to read long after I'm gone. That, my friends, is reaching higher. Right now the target is a long way off, maybe, but I'll bring the target closer by doing the very best I know to do until I reach that point and then I'll reach for another and another. Who knows how many books I'll write that will have a world changing affect on people? Right now I do not know that answer but I'll keep reaching until I do.

If you want to reach higher, think higher and become a person of wealth; go hang out with a millionaire, or better still, a billionaire, until you find out how they did it. Let them mentor you. The only reason people do not want to go higher is because they do not want to exert the strength it will take to climb the stairs of learning. They want a quick fix and ride the elevator to wealth. "Ain't gonna happen, Charlie. It just ain't' gonna happen." It's like riding a merry-go-round hoping that when (if) you get off, you'll get off at the right place. Keeping your fingers crossed and wishing for Lady Luck to do something is a waste of time.

Take the stairs, my friend, take the stairs. There is much to be learned. You can adjust your sights while on your way to the abundant life. Have no fear of the guy on the elevator getting there (wherever that is) before you and grabbing your "stuff". You'll always beat him because his elevator does not go all the way to the top. It's called delusion.

There Are No Days Off In Life

"There is no increase where there is no investment." Dr. B

If you did not invest in yesterday, there will be no returns today. If you do not make a deposit today, there can be no withdrawals tomorrow. If you want something tomorrow that you have never had before; then you must do something today that you have never done before, otherwise your tomorrows will be just like today. If I made no investments yesterday (I wasted it), today will be pretty much the same. It will be without purpose, passion and the pursuit of those things meaningful and necessary in life. There will be no positive returns. Here is a success tip for you; peak performers (giving their maximum every day) always win in the end. Those who perform with a "Ho Hum" attitude and approach to daily living will always lose in the end. Peak performance is an attitude that says, "I will give it all I have today. My success tomorrow depends on it. I must perform (positively) to the maximum that I can to earn the greatest reward and harvest at day's end."

I've watched people present their credit cards at the store or restaurant after making their purchase and it would be denied. Why? They probably were over their limit. They had not made the necessary payments allowing them to make future purchases. The guy says, "I want a raise and if you don't give me one, I'm outta here." "Well Bubba, I have some great news for you. There's the door, don't let it hit you on your way out. Buh-by, see ya. Have a nice day. I can't give you a raise when you've done nothing to warrant one." No investment, no raise. That's called simple arithmetic.

You see, that person invested nothing but wants everything to come his way. So it is with life, no investment, no withdrawals. You'll die young and your dreams will go with you to your grave, dead, having done nothing with your life or your dreams.

"How long will you slumber, O Sluggard? When will you rise from your sleep? A little sleep, a little slumber, A little folding of the hands to sleep – So shall your poverty come on you like a prowler, and your need like an armed man (Proverbs 6:9-11 NKJV)

How long will you let life go by without making an investment? How long will you sleep? How long will you wait on Lady Luck (whoever she is)? How many times should you cross your fingers hoping that everything will turn out all right? "I sure hope tomorrow turns out to be a better day. Today was a bummer; nothing good happened, same old stuff. I want to forget today ever happened." The Psalmist asks, "How long will you sleep?" How long will you deny the fact that everything is, in fact, working the way you ordered it? You said life was a bummer, so it is. You said nothing good happened and it didn't. You said you wanted to forget that day, since it was a waste anyway, so you will not be able to make a withdrawal from it; it is a closed account, a forgotten issue. You learned nothing from it.

One problem that arises if you continue to make withdrawals from an account that is already depleted is that you will come to a place of no return. You will wind up on the proverbial merry-go-round, going nowhere. Depression now has an open door; oppression sees the open door as an opportunity to do its thing, frustration and discouragement accompany and hosts of other "unwanteds" will soon overtake you. All hope has vanished. You are now on the devil's turf having made no sound investments in life. The day in which you made no investments now begins to multiply; one day leads into several, several days lead into weeks, several weeks into years and several years into a lifetime. Now it's too late.

You cannot afford to take a day off from life. People wonder why poverty suddenly appears in life. Most poverty (poverty is lack in any given area) is invited by the one who is complaining about everyone and everything, and changing nothing. Their words fall on shallow ground. Positive words that change lives and have world changing affects, go deep into the soil and soul of a human being and take root there; but negative words just lie on top of the soil taking no root and eventually die having accomplished nothing.

So it is with the empty, careless words of many people. Negative words make no positive deposits but positive words do because they change things around them. The whole atmosphere is charged when positive words are spoken. Not so with negative words. They have a devastating affect not only on the person speaking them but also on those around them. They have a negative impact while positive words have a positive impact.

Remember these words from Luke 6:38, "Give and it shall be given you." Here in this application, it doesn't apply to money; it could in other applications. Here, it applies to lifestyle, a way of living. But the Scripture does not stop there. Here is the good part. It goes on to say that when we give (invest) there is a return. What kind of a return? A return that is a good measure, it's pressed down, it's shaken together and it's a running over kind of return. Likewise, our giving should be in the same manner. When we give (invest in another) it should also be a good measure, pressed down, shaken together and it too, should be running over.

Giving should be a part of our daily lives. Peak performers are people with purpose and they are givers. They give it their all. I like to give all that I can to another so that they in return can give all they can to another. Eventually, it will come back full circle to all those who were givers. Everyone performs to the highest degree possible. They give their maximum today so that tomorrow they will have something to draw from. If a person is in a circle of giving people and one does not give it their all, they break the flow and someone gets cheated. Don't let that one be you.

If a person who is a peak performer takes a day or two off from training, they can tell very quickly that they are not able to give it their all. When peak performance is called for and demanded, they don't have it to give. I can remember several people who, when they took time off from their daily regime of training, found it very difficult to return to that regiment of training. One person I remember in particular had taken off several weeks from training. When he returned to "work out", it was "Katy, bar the door". He wasn't up to it and it took him several days before he was finally up to that point of strength that he left for a "time off". Was it worth the time off? Probably not, because it cost too much in the long run and the long run is what we're after. Don't take too much time off from life. Stay in it for the long haul, you'll be glad you did. It pays super dividends.

It is the same way with anything in life. If you have been doing something for any length of time and decide to take time off, for whatever reason, hoping to return to it at a later date, I have news for you. It probably isn't going to happen. It will take time, in some cases a long time, to regroup. The initiative and motivation will not be there.

It is the same way with going to church. If you have been a "regular" at your church and suddenly decide it is time to lie back for a while, you will find it nearly impossible to get back into your church routine and you will soon drop out altogether. Kids do that at school. They drop out for whatever reason, never to return. You can drop out in life and never return to what once was. You can drop out of relationships, too tired to make the grade, never to return. Many Christians do that. They drop out of their relationship with the Lord, never to return. That, my friend, is a very dangerous move. People drop out of life not having counted the cost of a severed relationship. It can be very costly. Don't let any one call you a dropout! If people are going to name you, let them name you a Winner!

People, who take too many days off from life and simply drop out of life, generally wind up living under a bridge. Seclusion is delusion and is not the answer to life's problems. Running from problems never solves them. The problems will continue to follow you, even under a bridge. Don't follow in the footsteps of people hiding from society under a bridge. How are they going to help you? It might go something like this, "Hey fella, uh, you there under the bridge; I have this problem and need some quick advice. What words of wisdom do you have for me so I won't become like you?" His response is likely to be, "You can't win out there, nobody does. Come on and join me. Live under a bridge with me and let life give you a few handouts because they sure won't give you a hand-up when you need one."

Ecclesiastes 9:10a (KJV) says, "*Whatsoever thy hand findeth to do, do it with thy might...*" This verse says it all. Whatever a day hands you, do all you can and do it with all your might. If it is a bummer, change it; make it a day of rejoicing. The Bible says that we are to count it all joy, the good times and the not so good times. We are to rejoice! Here is what we should look for every day, opportunity to rejoice in the Lord. Here is a great word study for you. The phrase, "good cheer" appears eight times in the Bible; the word "joy" appears 165 times, "rejoice" 192 times, "happy" 28 times, and "laugh/laughter" 25 times. So, BE HAPPY! If you must take time off from life for a day or two, then do it with all your might. Just remember to hurry back and get involved again with life. Change begins with you and me. The boss says to an employee, after an incident calling for some serious redirection, "Take a day off and think it over. Come back tomorrow with a better outlook and we'll start over again." The employee comes back to work the next day and sure enough, it's a better day for all concerned.

Colossians 3:23 (KJV) says, "*And whatsoever ye do, do it heartily, as to the Lord, and not unto men.*"

Rejoice, and again I say, rejoice!

Chapter Eighteen

Measure Life Correctly

"For with the measure you use, it will be measured to you." (Luke 6:38 NIV)

"Judge not, that you be not judged. For with what judgment you judge, you will be judged; and with the measure you use, it will be measured back to you." (Matthew 7:1-2 NKJV)

Isn't it amazing how we see other people? At first glance, we have them sized up and ready for the judgment of God and pronounce them as among the wickedest of all people. We don't take the time to get to know the person. We measure them, find they don't meet our criteria, and throw them out with the dirty bath water. We have become as little "gods" thinking we are doing the work of Almighty God; surely, this will find favor with God. Not so! We, in fact, bring the judgment of God upon ourselves. "Look at this one, God. Do you know what she's done? If I were you, I would throw this one out. After all, how useful could she be? I mean, I know some things about her that would make a sailor blush." (Read John 8:7) We go through life blindly with planks in our eyes, trying to take the speck out of another's eyes. But we have it in reverse. First, take the plank out of our own eyes. Then we can see clearly to help the other person.

One day I had stopped in at a fast food restaurant with a couple of other people for lunch. We got our food, found a place to sit, and began eating. During that time, one of the people in our group made this observation, "Bill, have you noticed that all the people in here are fat? They're fat, ugly and old. That happens, you know, when you come to these kinds of places." Of course, she forgot to mention the fact that she was 50 pounds overweight and I don't think she included herself in that group she was complaining about. It made me think of the times before that I had been in that same restaurant observing all the overweight people thinking, "I'll never get that fat. Never, ever, not even close to their condition. Yet, I was 35 pounds overweight myself. Wouldn't you say that is the pot calling the kettle black? I'll judge others but not me. It seems we have a tendency to call others what we already are but will not admit to. This is a very predominant thing in most churches. Those people are nothing more than religious robots going around correcting other people's faults, seeing none of their own. We're sent by God to help others, not condemn them.

In Matthew 7:3-5 (NIV) Jesus said, *"Why do you look at the speck of sawdust in your brother's eye and pay no attention to the plank in your own eye? How can you say to your brother, 'Let me take the speck out of your eye,' when all the time there is a plank in your own eye? You hypocrite, first take the plank out of your own eye, and then you will see clearly to remove the speck from your brother's eye."*

When I began writing this particular chapter, I found it to be the one in which I would struggle more than all the other chapters in this book. I had to ask the Holy Spirit why I was struggling so much. The words of this chapter came slowly, nothing would jell and I was floundering like a fish out of the sea. The anointing of God would come in spurts. It would come for a few seconds and then leave. I was in and out, up and down, until I realized this was an area in my own life that had to be dealt with and the Holy Spirit was not going to let me off easily. He chased me all over this chapter until I realized I had a problem and I needed God to help me through it.

Do you have a problem and God will not let you rest until it is dealt with? Are you judgmental, measuring others with worldly standards and not God's standards? Are you quick to take the speck from your brother's eye but have a log in your own?

I have great news for you. First, let God have the problem. Second, let Him walk with you through the problem and third, know that He will not abandon you with your problem but will with grace, mercy and love, help you through to the other side. Then and only then, will you be a help to others.

SUCCESS KEY - "Make every occasion a great occasion, for you can never tell when someone may be taking your measure for a larger place" (Marsden).

The problems we encounter through life are God's assignments to solve. When we get our own mess cleaned up, we are then qualified to help others out of their ditches; but until then, we must learn from our *own* problems. Don't be like the guy in Luke 18:11 who said (my words), "I'm sure glad I'm not like the rest of y'all." (He must have been a Southerner.)

Since we are digging, let's go a little deeper. You cannot find the gold in life until you start digging. And sometimes you just gotta go deeper, my friend, much deeper, to find the real gold. Don't be satisfied with the crumbs on the surface.

The Word says, *"But why do you judge your brother? Or why do you show contempt for your brother? For we shall all stand before the judgment seat of Christ.* (Romans 14:10 NKJV) Verse twelve (NKJV) reads, *"So then each of us shall give an account of himself to God."* Notice the word "himself". I am not accountable for any one else's actions; I am accountable for mine. I *will* be held accountable for every word spoken. Remember this, judgmental eyes always measure small. They do not see what God sees. He sees lives before and after. What we see is clouded by judgmental eyes, measuring wrongly, using worldly standards, all of which put stumbling blocks in the path of the other person.

WISDOM KEY - Don't put a stumbling block or a cause to fall in your brother's way. According to Matthew 18:6, you will be held accountable.

How many times have you measured a person (sized them up) only to find the measurements you took were not true. You looked at the external, measured, and walked off thinking, "I'm sure glad I'm not like them." You "dressed" them according to the way you perceived them; based on the external evidence presented and according to your own standards, not God's standards.

Isn't it amazing how we measure people not knowing that the measure we use for other people, will come full circle to haunt us in due time (See Matthew 7:1-5). We see some people richly dressed, that is, dressed up, but dead on the inside; yet we think them to be of great importance. We see others dressed down, (not so rich, not poor but not necessarily dressed up) yet rich on the inside. How we see others is generally how we see ourselves. If God were to reveal to us what we really look like in the mirror of life, we would not recognize our own selves. That's because we wear masks, hiding the real person. Jesus called those people hypocrites (play actors). The perception we have of ourselves is what we pass on in judgment of others. "I don't make enough money to dress like you, so if I can't have it, neither should you." "Who gave you the right to drive around in a luxury automobile while I have to drive around in this old jalopy? What's up with that?" The person who slams another person for driving a Cadillac isn't driving one himself. If he were, he would not slam the other person. It's what we don't have that causes us to look down our noses at others who have much. But it is not about what we have or do not have. It is perception, man's perception, and not God's. God simply sees all of us through a different pair of glasses. It's like the bifocals I wear. There are three areas that make up the lens; one for reading close, the second for reading far away and the third for reading in between close and far away. God sees us through His own glasses much the same way as I have described; the three areas that make up the lenses He looks through are: love, mercy and grace.

The way we measure another will surely come back to us according to Matthew 7:2. Another word for measure could be standard. The standard we use is all-important. Here are some critical questions to ask of our selves.

- Is the standard I use a high standard?
- Is it a Godly standard?
- When measuring another person, is it the same standard I would use to measure myself?

No, probably not. How would you like it if someone measured you according to the way you measured them? "Well, you don't have any right to have all that (whatever "that" is to you). After all, there are starving kids over in (you name the country) and they wouldn't be if they had what you have." Okay, let's turn that around. What if another person said the same about you? Would you be offended? You can bet your life you would be. "Hey, you don't have the right to say that about me." Why not? You said the same about them, didn't you? See how that works? You are fulfilling Matthew 7:1-5.

Don't judge unless you want to be judged likewise. Don't look to the outer man. Look for the good qualities in the inner man.

Jesus had much to say about the external versus the internal.

Here is what the Bible says in Matthew 23:27 (NIV), *"Woe to you, teachers of the law and Pharisees, you hypocrites! You are like whitewashed tombs, which look beautiful on the outside but on the inside are full of dead men's bones and everything unclean."*

What the religious sect of that day was doing, was par for the course. We do it even today. It's about people looking good on the outside for all to see, but rotten on the inside. Yes, even today many churches are filled with play actors. That is what the word hypocrite means; a person hiding behind a mask, an actor. You cannot see the real me if I am hiding behind a mask. We do that for attention from others. If we can get enough people to say something good about us relative to what they see externally, we think that will suffice for the misery we are living on the inside. Not so! Only Jesus can change that. To change the inside we must be born again (John 3:3). Then, and only then, will the change begin, and we will begin to measure correctly. The outer man will begin to change as the inner man changes and not one second before.

I see so many people today who look good on the outside but are miserable on the inside. They have measured life incorrectly and with wrong standards. I see this especially in the Church, mostly in non-denominational churches. They are all glitter and no gold, no place to go but show off. They have measured wrongly and will receive a measurement in like kind. It's even being done in many churches under the guise of "winning more souls" for Christ. What a lie! You don't need more money to win another person to Christ when that person lives next door. On a worldwide basis, yes, you would need all the resources available. But in either case, all you have to do is tell them about your experience (if you have one).

Luke 18:10-13 (NIV) says, *"Two men went up to the temple to pray, one a Pharisee and the other a tax collector. The Pharisee stood up and prayed about himself: 'God, I thank you that I am not like other men—robbers, evildoers, adulterers—or even like this tax collector. I fast twice a week and give a tenth of all I get.' "But the tax collector stood at a distance. He would not even look up to heaven, but beat his breast and said, 'God, have mercy on me, a sinner.'"*

This is another account of how two people measured them selves. One person saw himself from the outside (Wow, look at me!) while the other saw himself from the inside; a person who needed the grace and love of God to get him through one more day.

What standards are you using? What measuring device are you using? And remember, you cannot judge another for a thing when the same thing is going on in your own life. (See Matthew 7: 4-5) If the standards used are not God's standards, you will measure another incorrectly. You will short circuit the system. You will short change the other person putting a halt to what God has in store for them because you measured inaccurately. Romans 2:11 (NIV) says, *"For God does not show favoritism."* Another word for favoritism is standard. In other words, God uses the same standard for all people. Another word is partiality. God's love is unconditional so there is no "game" being played. What He says about one, He says about another. The ground is always level at the Cross.

If what you said about another were said about you, would you be pleased or offended? What have you said behind someone's back? If that person were brought before you, would you say the same thing to their face? You probably wouldn't because if it were true you would not have said it behind their back but to their face.

What God says about us and to us (whether we like it or not) is the same thing He would say to any other person. So don't be offended if God says something to you that causes you to cringe. If He is stepping on your toes, let Him do it. It is for our own good.

It seems I read somewhere that we are all in the same boat. Read Romans 3:23.

Let's talk about measuring. I have a mechanical and metal fabrication background of over 50 years. Over those years I've worked with some drawings that were over sixty years old. Even then, I could still build from those old drawings, the item described in detail on that drawing. There are other things besides dimensions on those drawings that are called standards and tolerances. It's what we would use to build the item on the drawing accurately.

Now here is what the word standard means, it is what we use to measure something by. It is regularly and widely used, a model to be used. It also means an upright support. It is something that is well established by rule or custom.

When we measure something, we probably would use devices either in the English or Metric system. There would be devices ranging from a 6" rule to a measuring tape, calipers and micrometers just to mention a few. They're established devices used to measure an item. Some of those items would measure in inches while others would measure more accurately in thousandths of an inch. All of these measuring devices, when properly used, will give us exacting measurements, telling us the size, length, diameter, thickness, width and other dimensions of the item being measured. These measurements give us a picture of a given item; they tell a story. These measurements can then be recorded on a drawing. From it we get a picture of what the item looks like. From the drawing we can reproduce the item. The item when finished should look just like the drawing.

All of this is a result of having used the right measuring device. If I do not use the right measuring device or standard, the measurements I get will not be a true picture of the item measured and I will wind up with something that does not and will not fit.

The Bible says that we are fearfully and wonderfully made in Psalms 139:14 (KJV). *"I will praise thee; for I am fearfully and wonderfully made: Marvelous are thy works; And that my soul knoweth right well."*

God took exacting and precise measurements to create us from using standards that were higher than our standards. He used His own image to create from. *"For my thoughts are not your thoughts,*

Neither are your ways my ways, saith the LORD. For as the heavens are higher than the earth, So are my ways higher than your ways, And my thoughts than your thoughts." (Isaiah 55:8-9 KJV)) "*And God said, Let us make man in our image, after our likeness: and let them have dominion over the fish of the sea, and over the fowl of the air, and over the cattle, and over all the earth, and over every creeping thing that creepeth upon the earth. So God created man in his own image, in the image of God created he him; male and female created he them. And God blessed them, and God said unto them, Be fruitful, and multiply, and replenish the earth, and subdue it: and have dominion over the fish of the sea, and over the fowl of the air, and over every living thing that moveth upon the earth." (Genesis 1: 26-28 KJV)*

For us to measure another person with standards other than those used by God Himself is to bring utter chaos upon ourselves.

God measured and then blessed us; we measure and curse God's creation. God measured and said go multiply. We measure and say, "You have no right to be blessed." God said, "Be fruitful." But we kill the fruit on the vine before it ever gets a chance to become all that it was created to be simply because we took wrong measurements and used devices contrary to the Word of God. We, as the title of this book implies, wear ourselves out by going around in circles.

I know of people who fabricated a product that was just "a little off" (on purpose) from what the client's drawings depicted. They thought no one would notice. The client said, "I want one of these and I will pay this amount for it." What they were saying is, "I want an exact duplicate of the item on this drawing." The fabricator took a short cut and gave the client what looked like the item he wanted, but in fact, was not. The client got cheated. Who got shortchanged? Both the client and the fabricator did.

We shortchange all concerned when we build to dimensions other than those on the original drawing. It's called the Word of God. The drawing (Word of God) has all the necessary dimensions from which to build the part. When we leave a dimension out, the part cannot be used for its intended purpose. When we leave grace out, the part is not whole. When we leave mercy out, the part is not whole. And certainly when we leave love out, the part is not whole.

God has a plan for you and me. His plan is in His Word (the Bible) and His Word will not return void. If you will get a picture of people through the eyes of God that is the Word of God, you will see clearly not only yourself, but others and then you will see God.

Chapter Nineteen

On a Hill Far Away

In this book, I've taken you around the mountain a few times. We've also crossed a few valleys, had a look at a few ditches, and in general, my plans for you in this book were, and are, to take you to higher places in life; to get you off the merry-go-rounds, get you out of the ditches and to help you through the valleys. My heart's desire is to get you headed up the mountain instead of you seeing the mountain as some kind of insurmountable place in your life. In other words, I do not want you to quit life just because a few obstacles got in your way.

I've talked about hills, valleys and mountains in this book on purpose. I've talked about how we go around in circles, wanting to climb the mountains, but because of our lack of faith in God, we never climb to higher heights. I could write for the next 100 years and not cover all the pitfalls in life. Hopefully, though, I've got you started in looking at life as something beautiful and you can, if you will try. I really do mean, try, to overcome anything that life hands you, with God's help, of course.

But before all this, there is something else I must talk to you about; it is your relationship with Jesus.

Let's go back a few years. My favorite hymn as a youngster in my old church, The People's Baptist Church in Bath, Maine, was, and still is, "The Old Rugged Cross". You remember those words, don't you? "On a Hill far away, stood an Old Rugged Cross."

Almost 2,000 years ago, a man climbed a hill that was far away and He succeeded in going to the top. It was no ordinary hill. It was called Golgotha. He did not receive the silver, the bronze or the gold medal for having made it to the top. There were no accolades. There were no "atta boys" and slaps on the back with a "Way to go, guy". There's even been a book written about it. It's called the Bible. Instead of the usual awards given to a person for having reached the top, this man was nailed to an Old Rugged Cross.

While we chase the accolades and rewards of man, Jesus was rewarded by man by being nailed to a cross for our sins. Redemption would be our reward through His death, burial and resurrection. Jesus' ultimate reward was that He conquered death, the world and sin and would ascend to the right hand of God, the Father. He did this for all of mankind. Because of His shed Blood on the Cross of Calvary, we have been redeemed and forgiven.

There is a higher place for all of us and it is found in Jesus. All you have to do is ask Him into your heart. You can start all over again by being born again into the family of God.

Psalm 61:2 (KJV) reads, "...when my heart is overwhelmed: Lead me to the rock that is higher than I."

Your relationship with Jesus, the Son of God, can begin today. Here is how you can be led to the "Rock" that is higher than you, a simple prayer.

Jesus, I know I am a sinner. Please forgive me and save me. Come into my heart right now. I want to be born again from above. I need you in my life as Lord and Savior. Jesus, I accept your plan for my life right now. I want to serve you as Lord of my life for evermore. In Jesus name, Amen!

If you prayed that simple prayer, you have been born again and Jesus now lives in you. Find a church home that preaches the Bible and begin your walk with Him to the place that is higher than I.

God Bless You!

Send me an email and let me know how I can help you. It's winnow@earthlink.net.

Other books by Dr. Seavey:
Journey to the Top

Future books:

God Loves a Winner
Teamwork
Adventures in Healthy Living
I was headed for a Ditch – But God
God, I'm Stuck Again Please Help Me
God, Please Renew My Mind
Power Thoughts for Powerful Daily Living
Lessons for Living
God, I Can't Make another Day without You
Come, Follow Me
Chosen to be Fruitful and Multiply
When the Mountains get too high to Climb
Shut up Alone with God
Devotional
You Can't Get Rich in a Ditch

TO ORDER PRODUCTS BY DR. SEAVEY:

Email winnow@earthlink.net or
Contact www.lluminapress.com or your local Barnes and Noble
bookstores.

About the Author

W.G. Seavey is founder of The Winners Circle Ministries. "It is my life's purpose and desire to help people out of the ditches of life and set them on higher ground. If I can help people win in the race of life, I have done well and served my purpose." TWCM is your *Wisdom Center* for successful living (Proverbs 3:1-27).

To contact Dr. Seavey for speaking engagements:

The Winners Circle Ministries
P.O. Box 14204
Humble, Texas 77347

Email: winnow@earthlink.net